Hold Fast and Stay True
Navigating the Dangers of Longevity in Ministry

John Harvey

Published by:

PANTHERA PUBLISHING
PANTHERAPUBLISHING.COM
STUART, FLORIDA

DEDICATION

This book is dedicated to my amazing wife, Alana, who has held fast and stayed true for 36 years of ups and downs, crazy ideas, a long-distance move, tears, and laughter. Without you, I would not be standing today!

To my incredible kids, Emily, Zach, and Kimberly, who lived through all the mess and the joys and loved me anyway! You were dedicated to God before you were born, and you belong to him for all of your days!

Preface

Having never written a book before, I certainly have never had to struggle with what to name a book. I thought about "Ramblings from a Rambling Mind," "My Journey to Confusion," or "Chronicles of Chaos," but none of those seemed quite right.

The purpose of this book, as stated in the Introduction, is to help people in ministry develop guardrails against some common issues that can cause people to have major difficulties in ministry or leave ministry altogether. I have watched over the last few years as friends and colleagues of mine have thrown in the towel or have been forced out of ministry because they did not have strategies to deal with the pitfalls that almost everyone in ministry faces. This book is designed to help you avoid those pitfalls and thrive in the ministry God has called you to oversee.

"Hold Fast" and "Stay True" are navigation terms used by sailors. To "Hold Fast" means that you maintain a tight grip on the lines of the sails, especially during a storm. Storms can be terrifying on a sailboat. You must "Hold Fast" to keep control of the vessel.

When I served in Haiti, our mission would routinely take teams to the island of Tortuga. Don't think

"Pirates of the Caribbean" and Captain Jack Sparrow. Think instead of devastating poverty and a desert surrounded by water. The boat we used, helmed by Captain Sebastian, was affectionately termed "The Jesus Boat." It looked like Jesus may have ridden on it, and it caused you to get closer to Jesus when you took it out on the water.

One Sunday, a group of doctors who were visiting the mission wanted to go to Tortuga for the experience. It was arranged, and they set sail. From the mission, we could see the sailboat as it headed across. We could also see the storm that came up, seemingly out of nowhere. For a couple of hours, we watched as Sebastian tried to keep the boat pointed toward Tortuga. We could imagine how everyone on board was dealing with this situation. The group made it to Tortuga but was stranded there overnight. When they returned the next morning, they had faces filled with relief, and stories of fear and doubt about their journey across.

"Stay True" is another term that means to keep going in the right direction. It is a term used in sailing and orienteering that means to stay moving in the direction the compass is pointing. If we don't keep moving where the compass is pointing, we can find ourselves in serious trouble. We may think we are a little off course, but the consequences can be deadly.

In 1979, Air New Zealand Flight 901 took off for a sightseeing flight over Antarctica. The flight plan for the trip had been altered before takeoff, and the pilots put in the coordinates of the new plan. What they did not know was that the plane was two degrees off from where it was supposed to be. That meant as they traveled, they were 28 miles off course. That doesn't seem like a big distance, but it became a tragic miscalculation.

As Flight 901 descended from the clouds, the pilots wanted to descend further to get a better look at the landscape. Because the clouds and snow made Mt. Erebus in Antarctica invisible, the pilots had no idea that changing course put them in the direct path of the mountain. Because they were two degrees off course, they flew directly into the mountain, killing all 257 people aboard.

In ministry, storms will come where we must "Hold Fast" to the promises and character of God. We must also "Stay True" to what he has called us to do in our ministry for Him. This book will hopefully help you to develop guardrails where you can "Hold Fast and Stay True" throughout your entire ministry career.

At the end of each chapter, there are two sections to work through: Hold Fast and Stay True. Hold Fast are the scriptures that address the topic of the chapter. If we are to truly hold fast in ministry, we must first hold fast to the truth of God's Word.

The Stay True section addresses questions and thoughts that require honest consideration. You need to be honest with God, others, and most importantly, yourself. If you want to put guardrails in place to thrive in ministry, you can't hold back what needs to be uncovered.

TABLE OF CONTENTS

Introduction

Once again, I found myself with the phone to my ear and pacing up and down the street in front of my house. This scene had played itself out repeatedly in the last few weeks. My phone would ring, and it would be an elder, a church member, or a member of one of the two families I was trying desperately to help. And every time, I picked it up and paced.

I had been on church staff for over 15 years, but this was the first major church crisis I was facing as the senior leader. It was not only a church crisis, but it was also deeply personal. An elder in our church, who was also a worship pastor and was leading our building campaign, was having an affair with another church member. Not only was he a church leader, but he was also my best friend. My family was very close to both families involved. Now I not only had to navigate the church through this pain, but I also had to manage myself and my heartbreak.

So, as each call came in, I answered, went outside, and paced. I was a wreck and had no idea how I would ever come out of this storm. What I couldn't see in all my pain and frustration was the toll this was having on my family, and the extra burden I was placing on them.

Most of these calls came in the evening when people were driving home from work and had some time to have a private conversation. Unfortunately, it was usually around dinner time for my family. I can feel all you are cringing. I wasn't consciously missing family dinners. I wasn't purposely missing helping kids with homework or just family time together. I wasn't blowing off my family for my own hobbies. I was trying to hold a church, two other families, and my sanity together. But it took a toll.

I would often come back in after everyone had finished dinner. I would warm up my dinner, eat in silence, and try to process the last conversation. My wife would do the dishes, my kids were doing homework or bath time, and I would collapse into a chair, emotionally and spiritually spent.

This all happened in the middle of my ten-plus-year tenure as a Lead Pastor. I wish I had a great ending to the story that included families being restored, repentance being asked for and granted, and a smooth, easy continuation of ministry. Instead, the couples divorced, the ones having the affair ran off to the other side of the country, people left the church, and our building program took a huge chunk of flesh. The building was completed, ministry moved on, life rolled along. And for all the time that has passed, my heart still breaks.

So many people find themselves at breaking points in ministry. Literally, before I sat down at my keyboard today, I was on the phone with a friend who said they were simply "tired of being on a church staff." When we got into ministry, we wanted to genuinely help people find Christ and grow in their relationship. What we didn't sign up for was sin, sin-inflicted crisis, disgruntled church members who dislike everything from the music to the temperature, and no one I know got into ministry to build as many buildings as possible. But all of these things are realities in the church in America.

As I sit over a decade removed from this situation, I have wrestled with all the mistakes I made. Here is a brief list of issues I have battled with over the last fifteen years.

I let other people's sin become my issue.

I thought my evening phone calls were a necessary evil of ministry.

I felt obligated to be available to everyone who wanted my time and attention.

I felt pressured to push on with physical projects instead of dealing with the spiritual life issues.

I thought I could handle it all.

Those are the ministry-focused side. But the BIGGEST regret, and the one I can't seem to forgive myself for, is allowing what I thought God had called me to overtake time with my young family. In that storm, I had a high school daughter, a middle school son, and an elementary daughter. Our lives were filled with various school and sports activities, serving in church together, and so much family fun and joy. But as I reflect on that season of life, I feel like I let my wife and our kids down.

This book is meant to help people recognize some traps in ministry that, if not addressed, may lead to you burning out and leaving ministry, or worse, losing your family in the process. After 36 years in ministry, my heart has a passion and a deep desire to help others miss the painful lessons I learned so that they can have thriving, joy-filled homes, families, and ministries.

I hope you press on through my tales of failure and learn the most important lesson that I needed in that season but didn't learn until much later....

"Jesus died for the church, so you don't have to."

I was convinced that if I didn't fix everyone's issue, if I didn't have the broadest shoulders and the best answers, everything would fall apart. As pastors, yes, we need to set the pace. We need to lead. We need to be the one pointing people back to Jesus. We need to open the scriptures and correctly explain the Word of God. But we are never called to sacrifice the most important ministry God has given to us, our family.

I have talked with my wife, Alana, and each of my kids about this season of my life and the mistakes I made. I have asked for forgiveness and been granted incredible grace. But I want to help others avoid my mistakes.

The remainder of this book is going to look at the life of Joseph and the lessons we can glean as modern-day ministers of the gospel. If you haven't read his story in Genesis in a while, this is a great time to revisit it. My prayer is that through scripture, life examples, and others' wisdom, we can find a roadmap to help pastors stay in ministry and thrive, not just survive.

I have spent the last year talking with pastors, student pastors, and church leaders to gain insight into what they see as important lessons learned over time. Each of the men and women I have talked with has over 20 years in full-time ministry. My prayer is that we can develop healthy rhythms in life and in ministry that will help us succeed, not just in the short-term, but in the eternal things that matter most.

Introduction

Chapter 1-Beginning at the End

"When I buy a new book, I always read the last page first. That way, if I die, I know how it ends?" Billy Crystal in "When Harry Met Sally"

"That's the person I want to become." We may not actually say it out loud, but we have thought it. They are at the pinnacle of their career. They have reached the top. Their family is strong, prominent, and everyone treats them with respect. They have power. When younger people look up to them, they dream of one day being as successful.

When we look at our world, even our Christian community, we see people who have had incredible success. They have large platforms, packed churches, and sell out arenas. Everyone knows their name, buys their books or music, and attends their conferences or concerts. But it wasn't always that way.

When I started in student ministry in the 1990s, one of the biggest conferences going in the American student ministry world in those days was the Dawson McAllister Conference. Dawson was a speaker, radio host, and author. He would travel around the country and host weekend conferences for teenagers.

Thousands of teenagers gathered at the largest churches in their cities to hear Dawson speak. We would load up vans, find churches in the area to let our youth group crash there for the night, and settle in for a fast-paced 24-hour journey. Those were incredible weekends.

One of the years I remember the most was not because Dawson was so incredible or that his teaching was so great. What I remember about that year was the new guy he brought out on stage to lead some worship songs. This young kid came out on stage wearing a cowboy hat and a Garth Brooks microphone, which was super cool at the time and now every preacher uses. He played his guitar and did a few songs. He was really good. He seemed like a great worship leader with a promising future. In fact, I have seen him in concert several times since. Chris Tomlin wasn't always the headliner. At one point, he was an add-on worship leader at another person's conference.

When you have been around as long as I have, you have seen names and faces in ministry come, go, rise, fall, and come back again. I have seen The Newsboys, Peter Furler edition, in giant arenas and packed music festivals. The first time I ever saw them play was in a church fellowship hall in Redlands, California, when they were still playing electro/dance music.

I have watched Tenth Avenue North win Dove Awards and play concerts. I hosted their very first concert in Stuart, Florida, for a student ministry weekend retreat. Drew Middleton, one of the OG's from Tenth Ave., was a student in our ministry at the same church.

It is sometimes easy to look at those who have had "success" and think, they have always had it made. But often what is missed is the struggle along the way. No one noticed Chris Tomlin waiting to get to another city to play three songs on the weekend and thought, "That dude's a star." No one saw the Newsboys load their gear into a dingy church basement and thought, "That's the life." No one saw me feed Tenth Avenue North pizza and pay them $200 bucks to lead worship for a group of 150 students and thought, "Those guys will headline one day."

On the flip side, everyone knows the story of the struggles of our subject for this book. Everyone knows about his coat, his brothers, his betrayal, his time in prison, and his feeling of being forgotten. But very rarely does anyone look at the ending of his life in such detail. So, before we get to the beginning, let's start at the end.

Genesis 50 reports...

> *"So Joseph and his brothers and their families continued to live in Egypt. Joseph lived to the age of 110. 23 He lived to see three generations of descendants of his son Ephraim, and he lived to see the birth of the children of Manasseh's son Makir, whom he claimed as his own. 24 "Soon I*

will die," Joseph told his brothers, *"But God will surely come to help you and lead you out of this land of Egypt. He will bring you back to the land he solemnly promised to give to Abraham, to Isaac, and to Jacob."* **25** *Then Joseph made the sons of Israel swear an oath, and he said, "When God comes to help you and lead you back, you must take my bones with you."* **26** *So Joseph died at the age of 110. The Egyptians embalmed him, and his body was placed in a coffin in Egypt."*

By the time we get here, we are so tired of the story of Joseph, most of us just skim over this section and move on. But there are some major implications there that I want us to look at before we get to the rest of Joseph's life.

This passage tells us that Joseph lived to be 110 years old. When we first meet him, he is a boastful, dreaming young man of seventeen. He is unmarried, unfettered, and unappreciated. Now, ninety-three years later, he is the second in command of the largest empire in the world at the time. I wonder if the seventeen-year-olds of the day knew of his beginnings. Did they know his brothers tried to kill him? Did they know he was a former slave? Did they know he was sent to prison?

In our current era, we can simply look up any person from any point in history and get their full life story. Here are a few interesting facts about well-known people:

Leonardo da Vinci was an animal rights activist. He would buy caged birds in markets just to set them free.

Henry Ford tried to stop World War I by going to Europe to meet with peace activists who were gathered to try to convince Europe to avoid a war. When he landed, he was met by only eight college students.

Leo Fender, who perfected the electric guitar, couldn't play the guitar and hated rock and roll.

Ed Headrick, who invented the Frisbee, had his ashes molded into Frisbees and left them to his family.

The list of crazy facts we can find goes on and on. Usually, what we know of someone is how their life ended up, not how they got there. With Joseph, the reverse is true. We know most about how he got to where he ended up, but we don't spend much time on that part of the story.

It's only 4 verses of scripture. We meet Joseph in Genesis 37, and most of the rest of Genesis is spent on his life. But these four verses offer glimpses that we may miss because they are not as spectacular of a tale.

It is not until verse 23 that we find out that Joseph had a wife and children. It tells us he lived to see three generations of descendants of his son Ephraim. That means he saw his grandchildren, his great-grandchildren, and his great-great-grandchildren. Not many people got to see their great-great-grandparents.

Because this is a society based in oral tradition and because of who Joseph was, can you imagine the stories Ephraim told his sons about his dad? They must have thought they were all made up and couldn't possibly be real.

I have heard crazy stories about my grandfather my whole life. I have heard how when my dad was six years old, my grandmother put him and my uncle in an orphanage in Mississippi. I heard how my grandfather and his brother broke into the orphanage one night and literally kidnapped my dad and uncle out of the orphanage. I always wondered if Mississippi was still looking for my dad!

I heard how my grandfather invented the starter for an automobile and how he tried to get Ford Motors to buy his invention. Instead, the next year, Ford introduced a car that could start from the inside.

Those pale in comparison to Joseph's life. When Joseph was 110 years old, it was probably hard to distinguish what was real and what sounded impossible. Except that his brothers, who set these events in motion, were alive to confirm the stories.

Joseph never saw Egypt as his home. Even at the end of his life, achieving all he had achieved in Egypt, Joseph still recognized he was a foreigner in a foreign land. He did not want his body to be left in Egypt. Instead, he wanted to be buried in the same land as his people when they left Egypt.

We are never told that Joseph had any special insight into how long his people would be in Egypt. He probably assumed that he famine would end and they would soon return to the land of his forefathers. I would guess he had no idea that it would be 430 years before one of his descendants, Moses, would lead the nation out of Egypt. But as he did, he made good on the promise that Joseph would be buried with his people.

"Moses took the bones of Joseph with him, for Joseph had made the sons of Israel swear to do this. He said, "God will certainly come to help you. When he does, you must take my bones with you from this place." Exodus 13:19

After 523 years, Joseph's journey ended where it started. With all the pain, all the heartache, all the betrayal, and all the power of his life, Joseph ends where we all do, as dust in the ground.

The main point I want you to get from this opening passage is that all of our lives are made up of stories, adventures, and dramas. And while we are living them, we have very little comprehension of what history will say about us. We move from season to season and hope that we are following as hard after Jesus as possible. We pray that when we die, we would have made a difference in the world and in the Kingdom of God. And for most of us, our lives will never be recorded in history books, and our legends will fade away with us.

My prayer is that we may live our lives in such a way that, while the masses may not know who we are, the heavens will be filled with the voices of the lives we have impacted. This book is designed to help you journey well through your ministry life and build in guardrails that will help you last for decades. And in doing so, the impact of our lives will be felt for generations.

So, let's look at the life of Joseph together. Let's learn from his journeys and seasons. Because at some level, we will face them as well. Every issue Joseph faced is still an issue in our lives today. And if not managed well, they will cause us to fall short of the plans and purposes God has ordained for us.

Hold Fast

How do your dreams line up with the dreams spoken of in Joel 2:28-32?

Stay True

If someone asked you what your dream would be for your ministry, what would be your answer?

Does your answer involve metrics, i.e., number of people, dollars raised, buildings built?

How have you prepared yourself to attain your dream?

What would your life look like if you fulfilled your dream?

Chapter 1-Beginning at the End

Chapter 2- Family

"Ohana means family, and family means no one gets left behind or forgotten."

Lilo and Stitch

Everyone has a family. That may seem like an obvious statement, but our family is the first imprint on our lives. The family we were born into shapes how we see God, how we see others, and how we see the world. Whether you are born into a loving, healthy family with two awesome parents, or you were given up for adoption the moment you hit the earth, your family leaves a lasting imprint.

I was born into what looked like, on paper, a typical American family. My parents, Charles and Mamie, already had five kids, and I rounded out the bunch seven years after the youngest. I was, for sure, the unplanned oops! But in my early life, my family life was great.

I don't ever remember living in the house with my two oldest brothers. They had moved off to college by the time I really started to remember. But they were around at various times. Our house was a hub of activity. Growing up in the OakHaven neighborhood of Memphis, Tennessee, in the 1970s was a dream. We attended the same church and school as everyone else, we rode our bikes all day in the summer until the street lights came on, and every house had a water hose available for a quick refreshing drink...You just had to remember to let the hose run for a few minutes or else the fire coming out would burn your lips!!

During those years, there were some dynamics in my house I was too young to understand. Finances were always tight. We didn't have enough for a ton of extra things, but we always had plenty of food and people around. Around this same time, an event happened that imprinted my life for decades.

I had always been close to my mom, I guess the way any six-year-old is. We would take walks around the neighborhood, she would fix my favorite meals, and her car never seemed to pass an ice cream shop without turning in. But one day, something changed.

We were visiting some family friends in the neighborhood. All the older kids had matching siblings in the other family, but I was the youngest and after a while I was kicked out of every other room in the house by the older kids. I went and sat down in the living room and could see my mom and her friend talking in the kitchen as they cooked dinner. While I could see and hear them, they did not know I was there. I overheard my mom make a statement that I didn't fully understand in the moment, but that has haunted me for decades. She said, "If I had my choice, we would have stopped at five kids."

As soon as she said it, she turned and made eye contact with me. In that moment, she immediately began to say how she would never have wanted not to have her little one. You know how people react when you catch them in something? That was what I saw my mom do for the first time in my life. It was also the first time that math became easy for me. Six minus five is one, and I was that one!

Before you go too far down the road, I want you to know that my mom and I came to have a good relationship. It was not perfect because we were two imperfect people. But I do believe that my mom loved me. We will discuss this more a little later.

My point in sharing this story is to help us establish the fact that our family life imprints us in ways we may never understand in the moment, or for that matter, decades. For the next three decades, my life was shaped by a feeling of being unwanted, in the way, and needing to prove my worth. It impacted how I related to friends, how I related to females in my life, and my sense of understanding of God's love for me.

In the next few chapters, we are going to be looking at the life of Joseph in scripture. Joseph is one of the few people in the bible that you can look at their life and not see major sin and failure. He never killed anyone, he never committed adultery, he never lied to protect himself. He lived a life of incredible integrity and faithfulness to God. But in all of this, he experienced some crazy moments that shaped him. Joseph had his own issues with his family. While he never had to question his parents' love for him, he did have to deal with the effects of that relationship. His story begins in Genesis 37, and right away, there are some details of his family life that should give us pause.

> *"When Joseph was seventeen years old, he often tended his father's flocks. He worked for his half-brothers, the sons of his father's wives Bilhah and Zilpah. But Joseph reported to his father some of the bad things his brothers were doing."* Genesis 37:2

First, we need to realize Joseph is 17 years old. He is not a small child, but he is also not fully a man on his own. He is still living as one of 12 brothers and dealing with how his father, Jacob, treated him compared to how he treated his brothers. Joseph is dealing with relationships out of his control. He is not fully from the same bloodlines as his older brothers. This creates tension in and of itself. In the time of Jacob, blessings, inheritance, and possessions were handed down and given to children in a certain order. The oldest child received the full blessing of his father, and the other brothers were left to a lesser portion. Being a stepbrother brought its own set of challenges. If you were a favored son and liked to rat out your brothers, life was even more eventful!!

Joseph's brothers were doing things that would not have made their father happy. Jacob was a godly man who sought to follow God's plan and ways as much as possible. It is important to remember that at this time, there was no written law and no scripture. And the Holy Spirit was not yet dwelling in the hearts of men.

But Jacob would have known, and would have passed down to his sons, the promises and the stories that were passed to him from Abraham and Isaac. He would have told them about God's call to their great-grandfather. He would have told them about Abraham leaving his family and his country and settling in the land. He would have told them about how God showed up to his grandfather and promised an heir, even though Abraham and Sarah were old and had passed childbearing years. He would have told them about how God provided a ram so that Abraham did not kill Isaac. Surely, he would have told them about how Lot was spared from Sodom and Gomorrah and how Lot's wife looked back and was turned to salt. What they would have known were the promises, faithfulness, character, and justice of God.

But, it says, "Joseph reported the bad things his brothers were doing."

We've all been there. As the youngest of six kids, I understand about blaming others. Siblings always pass the buck. The brother closest to me is seven years ahead of me. So, for me, David was the one whom I blamed everything on. If the grass wasn't cut, it was David's fault. If the cake batter was missing, David ate it, although I had a lot of stomachaches at that time. If a hole ended up in a wall or door because we were wrestling, it was David's fault. It took my sister thirty years to admit that she, and not my younger sister, had messed up the door on my dad's car.

My own children were no different growing up. Emily blamed Zach, Zach blamed Kimberly, and Kimberly had no one to blame but the dog whenever someone was getting in trouble. This resulted in her getting in trouble much less than she probably should have! Passing the buck and tattling on siblings is an age-old reality of families.

When we are imprinted by our family as a child, when we become an adult, those imprints show up in ways we never expect. My parents rarely attended my sporting events or school events. They literally saw me play one game of high school baseball. There were a lot of reasons and a lot of issues going on in their own lives, but their absence was a challenge for me. When my kids came along, I was probably too involved. I would show up at practice, sit through rehearsals, and be as involved as I could. My oldest daughter, Emily, had to tell me to stop showing up at her high school basketball practices because her teammates thought I was another coach. I was, in fact, a little too involved.

Family is a delicate balance to say the least. But when you add on the pressure of ministry, family life takes on a completely new set of challenges. As I stated in the introduction, I failed tremendously at this area for a season. I carried the weight of everyone else's burdens. I believed that if the church was going to succeed, I had to make it happen. Someone told me recently that, "Good pastors will do everything for a church, but a good church won't let him."

When I was the Lead Pastor, I had a season where I was also the student pastor, the worship leader, and the main speaker. My wife ran the children's ministry, my teenage daughter led worship when I wasn't, and I did all the other things pastors must do. I saw this as necessary because no one else stepped up. I should have put the brake on certain things, but I had a warped sense of what was "necessary."

What I could not see in that moment was the time I was stealing from my family. It was not intentional. I never set out to ignore my family time or to not be fully present. But the choices I made demonstrated, at certain seasons of my life, ministry was a mistress.

Every person who has served in ministry has had to face times of compromise of family time and presence. Of course, sometimes we must make bigger sacrifices. When there is a medical emergency or death, we can't simply sit it out. We must be present to meet others' needs. At the same time, these should be exceptions, not the rule.

For me, it was never sitting in my office and being a workaholic that caused tension in my family. In fact, I have been blessed to have jobs where I can be at ball games, practices, and theater performances. I may have made it to the games, but often it was time at home that slipped through my fingers. It was the dinner conversation, the evening game, the wrestling with my kids on the floor, or even just the gentle stroking of my daughter's hair as she downloaded the day that I often missed.

We often fail to see that when we cheat our family of our full attention, focus, and time, we are cheating the first ministry we have been called to oversee. In his book, "Choosing to Cheat," Andy Stanley says, "The problem is there is not enough time to get everything done that you are convinced-or others have convinced you, needs to be done." (2) Andy goes on to say that we will either cheat our jobs, or we will cheat our family. And he concludes that it is better to cheat your job and not your family. Losing a job is much less of a loss than losing your family.

This is not an excuse for poor work performance, laziness, or inefficiency. Instead, it is a call to an alignment of values and priorities. In cheating our job, or ministry, or time, we are simply saying we don't work unreasonable hours, and we don't put our family on the back burner. Instead, we do an honest day's work, and we fulfill our obligations. Then, when we get home, we are fully present, mentally available, and emotionally stable.

I have a friend named Jay who is a student ministry stud. This guy may be one of the smartest, organized, strategic men I have ever met. He has been in his current position for over 17 years. He also has been a widower, had a child with special needs, and another child with cancer. Jay has had as much tragedy and pain in his life as anyone I have ever known. Yet, he remains incredibly faithful.

When his first wife died, he had a three-year-old daughter and was a student pastor in West Virginia. He knew he needed a new start for himself and his daughter. So he left his job and relocated to Nashville for a time. He knew that he needed to be present for his daughter in a way that his current ministry context would not allow for.

Jay eventually moved to South Florida, married a wonderful Christian young lady, started a new ministry position, and continued to raise a family. Fast forward a few years, and one of his sons, Elijah, developed cancer. Medical treatments, medical bills, the uncertainty of the future, and the pain of watching his child suffer were everyday realities in his life.

On top of all those issues, his adopted daughter has some very serious intellectual, emotional, and behavioral issues that, at times, have seemed to be overwhelming. But Jay and Emily have remained faithful servants. And their church has been amazing in supporting and loving them. In fact, one of the things Jay told me is that his church is "awesome at pastoring the pastors."

Over some great BBQ one day, Jay and I were discussing the lessons God has shown him through all of this. Jay had a perspective shift over the years that has led to a mindset that every pastor needs to understand,

"You are replaceable at church. You are irreplaceable at home."

If more pastors and leaders understood this truth, I believe we would have healthier family relationships, healthier boundaries in place, and we would be more effective in ministry. We should expect that life is going to be challenging. Jesus told us in John 16:33, "I have told you all this so that you may have peace in me. Here on earth, you will have many trials and sorrows. But take heart, because I have overcome the world."

Jay shared with me his philosophy of ministry that not only impacts his life but is true of every minister: "Work as if you have a special needs child at home, because you do."

What he means is not that everyone will have a child with cancer or developmental issues, of course. But everyone in ministry who has a family has a child at home who has needs that only their father or mother can meet. Every boy needs his father to show him what it means to be a Godly man. Every daughter needs a mom to help her understand what it means to be created in God's image. Maybe you are unmarried, but you have parents who need you to be an active part of their lives. Maybe you simply want to be a good sister or brother. Ministry can create a barrier, if we let it, that limits our availability to our family. In my own experience, we often could not afford to travel to see Alana's parents in Texas, or we simply could not find someone to cover our responsibilities while we were away.

You are the only person your wife should find unconditional love, grace, and emotional stability from in her world. You are the only wife your husband should find the honor, respect, and intimacy he needs. You are the only man that your son should hear the lessons all young men need to learn as they step from childhood to adolescence to adulthood. And you are the only daddy or mommy your daughter needs to show her how she should be loved, valued, and honored. You are a valuable son or daughter, sister or brother to your family. When we don't fulfill those roles in our family's life, we invite a fallen, pagan world to become the leading influencer in our family.

Bob Pierce, who founded World Vision in 1950, was a legendary figure in the Christian relief movement. He traveled around the world to areas impacted by poverty, disease, natural disasters, and war. Everywhere he went, he brought not only lifesaving care, but the gospel of Jesus. He also founded Samaritan's Purse in 1970. What an incredible legacy!

Bob Pierce preached crusades through China and Korea before the communists took over. He traveled through India, Europe, and around the world, sharing the gospel and caring for those in need. One of his famous quotes is, "Break my heart for the things that break the heart of God." Dr. Pierce is also famous for saying, "I have made an agreement with God that I'll take care of His helpless lambs overseas if He'll take care of mine at home."

Bob would travel for 10 months out of the year and then be home for two. In talking with his daughter, Marilee Pierce Dunker, she remembers that when he would arrive home, he would take the family to a trip to Disneyland, and then he was back at his office and making movies to promote the ministry of World Vision. He would speak at crusades, he would do radio interviews, he would help raise money for the mission. But even when he was "home," he was not really home. Marilee described him as a "personality rather than a presence" in the family home.

Marilee has written a book, "Man of Vision" (Originally published as "Man of Vision, Woman of Prayer) (3), that describes how growing up as Bob Pierce's daughter shaped her life and how it impacted her mom and her sisters. While Bob was a larger-than-life figure in the world and the Christian community, his family at home was falling apart. His wife, Lorainne, suffered from incredible depression and really suffered from agoraphobia as she got older. The oldest sister, Sharon, suffered from deep insecurities, but she was a young woman who was very sensitive to the pain of others. She would take in an unwed mother, or she would help a friend down on her luck. Sharon married young and had a doomed marriage of four years. She took her own life when she was 27 and had asked the question, "Why does Daddy love all the children of the world, but not me?'

It is easy to hear those stories and to blame Bob Pierce for not caring for his own family. However, on many levels, each of us is guilty of putting our ministry, our ego, and our calling ahead of our family. Bob Pierce was an incredible man, who lived an adventurous life, and who did the best he could with what he knew. In his time and culture, no one stepped forward to challenge his perspective or his method. Everyone just saw him as the giant Bob Pierce.

How often do we want others to see us as giants in our field? Don't we want to be experts and have a name that others speak of with great admiration? The question we must always ask is, "At what cost?"

Marilee quotes Dr. Jack Hayford as saying that Bob suffered from the "evangelical syndrome." This is the mistaken idea that a man can only serve God to the fullest if he is willing to put his ministry before his family. Marilee recalls hearing her father quote Luke 14:26,

> *"If you want to be my disciple, you must, by comparison, hate everyone else—your father and mother, wife and children,*

brothers and sisters—yes, even your own life. Otherwise, you cannot be my disciple."

While Marilee didn't have her own father present for much of her life, she found a father figure when she and her husband, Bob Dunker, were on staff at Church on the Way in Los Angeles in the early 1970s. Jack Hayford, the loving, caring pastor for decades, took her under his wing and became a father figure. As her husband and she ministered to the young adults, they simply took their children along. When Bob Dunker left church ministry for Christian radio, Marilee stayed home with the kids and led ladies' Bible studies. It wasn't until her kids left her house and were on their own that she reconnected with World Vision and became a writer and ambassador.

World Vision sent Marilee around to speak to staff in different parts of the world. Her main role was to remind them to put their family ahead of the ministry. She told me that one time, while she was leading a staff retreat and talking about this topic, one of the wives of a staff member asked, "Do they know you are telling us this?"

In conversations with various people about this book, a common theme brought up by many I interviewed was that if the enemy can't get to you, he will attack your family. So often our family pays the price for our ministry. They see the ugliness of church conflict. They feel the weight of a difficult decision about how we spend the little amount of money we make. They often are on the losing end of the time we invest.

So, what do we do to protect ourselves and our families? This book is not a ten-step guide to lasting ministry. Instead, I want to invite you into some reflection and some conversations to help you build guardrails for yourself and your family. At the end of each chapter, I will provide you with a few practical steps to evaluate where you are in safeguarding yourself against these pitfalls.

Hold Fast

Read Matthew 1:1-18. What do you learn from the genealogy of Jesus as it relates to family?

Stay True

Here are some thoughts to think about as you develop a "Family First Ministry."

Conduct a time audit of the last three months. Pull out your calendar and account for every night out, every weekend meeting, and every "off hours" phone call. Ask these questions:

Were these all "necessary?"

Were there obligations placed on you by others? (If you didn't do them, would you lose your job?)

What family time did you miss because of these?

Thought: If you don't control your calendar, someone else will. Just because someone asks for a meeting at a certain time, you don't have to take it.

Share your time audit with your spouse? Ask them these questions:

Was there a time in this period that you were upset, angry, hurt, or disappointed that I was gone?

How do you think I am doing at putting our family first?

What can I do to help you know that you are my first ministry?

This is not about guilt but understanding. Don't be defensive. Don't make excuses. Just listen and learn.

Include your family in setting your agenda for the next three months.

Agree on how many nights out is realistic and healthy in your current life moment.

Agree on how many overnight trips (i.e. camps, mission trips, retreats, etc.) are healthy for your family.

Share your findings with your direct supervisor. Yes, this is scary, but not as scary as losing your family.

Tell them you are trying to be the best spouse, parent, and staff member you can be.

Ask if there are ways to adjust to certain meetings or expectations to safeguard your family.

Ask them to help you understand the areas that are non-negotiable and what is flexible in your ministry.

Chapter 2- Family

Chapter 3- Pride

"It is better to lose your pride with someone you love rather than to lose that someone you love with your useless pride." John Ruskin

I am going to admit something to you that most people I tell find incredible. They simply can't believe it to be true. They think I must be joking or exaggerating, but I assure you the next five words I am going to say are the complete truth..............I CAN'T STAND TOM CRUISE!

Shocking, right? I mean, he is the action star of all action stars. He is handsome, does all his own stunts, and has made some of the biggest movies in recent memory. I still don't care. I have never seen a Mission Impossible movie with Tom Cruise. The only exception to this rule is early Tom Cruise: Taps, The Outsiders, Top Gun, A Few Good Men, and Top Gun: Maverick. (Okay, yes, I know it is a newer movie, but it is a sequel, and so I had to see it.)

Other than that, Tom is not in my viewing habit. Here is the one thing that makes me not want to watch his movies is that I think he believes all the "stunts" he does are the real deal. I always have the feeling that he actually thinks he is Maverick or Ethan Hunt. I often feel like he can't separate his real self from his on-camera self. Honestly, I just think he is too full of himself.

I know this may be an unpopular opinion. I know most movie stars see themselves as better than or more capable. I get it. But for me, I can't get past my perception. I also know that Tom Cruise has no idea who I am. And honestly, he couldn't care less.

Sometimes in ministry, it is easy to believe the hype about ourselves. People tell us we are doing a good job, we are the experts in our field, and we gain a little following. And when that happens, we can begin to believe the hype. One of the dangers of people talking about you is you can begin to believe what everyone is saying. And that is not always a good thing.

> *"Jacob loved Joseph more than any of his other children because Joseph had been born to him in his old age. So, one day Jacob had a special gift made for Joseph— a beautiful robe. 4 But his brothers hated Joseph because their father loved him more than the rest of them. They couldn't say a kind word to him. 5 One night Joseph had a dream, and when he told his brothers about it, they hated him more than ever. 6 "Listen to this dream," he said. 7 "We were out in the field, tying up bundles of grain. Suddenly, my bundle stood up, and your bundles all gathered around and bowed low before mine!" 8 His*

brothers responded, "So you think you will be our king, do you? Do you actually think you will reign over us?" And they hated him all the more because of his dreams and the way he talked about them. 9 Soon Joseph had another dream, and again he told his brothers about it. "Listen, I have had another dream," he said. "The sun, moon, and eleven stars bowed low before me!" 10 This time he told the dream to his father as well as to his brothers, but his father scolded him. "What kind of dream is that?" he asked. "Will your mother and I and your brothers actually come and bow to the ground before you?" 11 But while his brothers were jealous of Joseph, his father wondered what the dreams meant." Genesis 37:3-11

Sometimes, we are our own worst enemy. Now I don't know too many people who have gone into ministry thinking that we will get a "beautiful robe" or because we think we will "rule" over others. But I have seen that acknowledgement, "success" in ministry, or accolades can change us.

In my first ministry, I came in as a 21-year-old who was handed the keys to a student ministry of six students. It was a part-time job while I was finishing my senior year of college. I had no plans to go into ministry. I was going to work at this church while

Alana finished her education, and then we would get married, and I was going to head to law school.

Over the next few months, we built great connections with the church and with the students. We started to see some new students show up, we saw students get serious about their faith, and the church was doing great. When I graduated in the spring, they offered me a full-time job. Alana and I got married in August, and she had a semester of school left. I told the church I would take the position with the understanding that I would probably be leaving when Alana got a full-time job.

When the time came for me to think about law school, I didn't even want to think about it. My heart had changed, and I loved being the pastor to students. We decided that this was where we felt God had led us, and we were ready to stay. The church was exciting, and we were ready for this new adventure to really crank up.

Our student ministry was growing. The senior pastor, Bill Walthall, and I developed a great relationship. He never saw me as some youth guy, but as a pastor. He brought me into elder meetings, I was included in planning and decision-making, and I got to preach much more often than any of my friends in ministry. The church then offered to pay for me to get my master's degree. I felt on top of the world.

What I didn't see was what this success was doing in my own heart. I became the guy who had all the answers, who was leading in areas others didn't understand, and who was the expert in the next generation. I was all of 24 years old.

In seminary, I met a man named Gary Stanley who became not just a professor but even a mentor to this day. Gary and his wife, Luci, attended our church and would, on occasion, chaperone a youth outing to Magic Mountain. Gary was also the preaching and public speaking expert at the seminary. So, every time I spoke at church, there was my professor sitting front and center. It was hard not to try to impress.

Over the next couple of years, as I continued my education, our ministry was exploding. I was on local school campuses, we were seeing student leaders on campus come to know Christ, and I was well-known in the community. I spoke at camps, became the guy leading a local student pastor network, and overall, was killing it! At least on the outside.

Inside, I was a mess. Every childhood insecurity haunted me every day. I was looking for validation and belonging everywhere. And I could not see my own pride. Andy Stanley said, "Pride and greed cannot see themselves in the mirror." What I didn't know, because everything looked great on the outside, was that pride and insecurity are two sides of the same coin. Just as Joseph had dreams that led him to pride and ego, I projected a confident (PRIDEFUL!) exterior to mask my inner insecurity. And it almost cost me my family, my ministry, and my reputation.

I had an encounter with Christ that shook me to my core. I had to confess sin, I had to get honest with my pastor and elders, and I had to get right with Alana. In the process of all of these issues, I began to experience panic attacks, depression, and felt like I should not ever have been born.

On one extremely difficult night, my wife called Gary and Luci at 2:00 in the morning. I was in a mess. I was crying, I was shaking and could not get myself calmed down. Gary and Luci showed up at our house with a guitar and immense grace. Gary played worship music, and we sang, and they prayed deep, powerful prayers over my life.

This was in my last year of graduate school. Our ministry was flourishing at the time, and our pastor was talking to me about taking over for him when he retired in a few years. It was a perfect storm of chaos and pressure. Those factors, and some poor, sinful choices I had made, created a perfect storm. But why?

What I realized was that the words I had heard years before from my mom had driven deep stakes of doubt into my heart. I needed to prove myself in every area. I needed to show I was valuable. It is a crazy paradox, but pride and insecurity often flow from the same spring in our heart.

Right before I graduated with my master's degree, I sat down for coffee with Gary. He made the most profound observation that I have ever heard. As we talked, he said, "When you came to seminary, you were a proud, arrogant young man with potential. You relied on your talent and ability to succeed." Not the ringing endorsement you hope for from your professor. Then he continued... "but now, you have done the hard work of connecting your heart with the true heart of God. Now, God can use you like never before."

Those words spoke life to me. I felt like God had led me through darkness I could never imagine and was delivering me into a new light. When I look at Joseph's story, I have always wondered why he told his family of his dreams. Was he an arrogant teenager? Was he trying to rub it in his brother's faces that he was favored? Was he simply a jerk?

There are a few truths we need to understand. Joseph was a teenager when he had these dreams. We have no writing or information to tell us that he fully understood them. He simply imagined that one day his family would bow to him. That makes for an awkward Thanksgiving celebration.

Joseph also firmly believed that his dreams would come true. Scripture doesn't tell us that God showed up to Joseph and told him about these dreams. But Joseph obviously believed that they had some divine backing.

We also know that these dreams were imprinted on Joseph. I believe that Joseph held his dreams through all of the pain and trials he experienced. I can imagine Joseph sitting in the cistern and thinking about how this moment played into his dreams. While he was a slave, I am sure Joseph held onto the idea that this was not his ultimate destiny.

The one area where we may see sin in Joseph's life was in the area of pride. Maybe his dreams fueled a pride in him. Maybe he felt like he had a destiny that set him above others. Maybe he simply felt like tending flocks and being an agrarian was simply not his path. In any sense, I think Joseph had to deal with pride as he walked through the events of his life.

Pride becomes one of those issues that can take us where we don't want to go. It can take what is good and useful and turn it into blocks that we must overcome to really be the people God has called us to be. Pride can blind us to our own frailty and shortcomings. Pride shows up in all kinds of ways. We think we are doing better than everyone else. We have all the answers that no one else has. We are the ones doing it the "right" way. Pride keeps us from being teachable. And pride is always lurking around the corner.

The Bible has 160 verses on pride. As you can imagine, most of them warn of the dangers of pride.

> *"Though the Lord is great, he cares for the humble, but he keeps his distance from the proud." Psalm 138:6*

> *"The Lord tears down the house of the proud, but he protects the property of widows." Proverbs 15:25*

"The Lord detests the proud; they will surely be punished" Proverbs 16:5.

God hates pride. And for the rest of our lives, we will have to seek to kill pride in our own hearts. It is so easy to step back and think we have it all together and we are killing it in ministry. The reality is that whether we are trapped in pride at the moment, or whether we are walking with humility with God, any blessing in our ministry is a result of God's work. If God is working in people's lives and hearts, even a sinful leader will not hold God back.

It is amazing to see how Joseph's pride in his youth, led him to being placed where God could use him in his old age. While I must continually check my own heart and my own mind, I have learned lessons that are giving me the ability to help younger pastors and leaders along the way. God has a way of redeeming our sin and our shame when we repent and confess before him.

Hold Fast

What does Psalm 101:5 teach you about dealing with your pride?

Stay True

Do a Pride Self-Check- Are You Filled with Pride or Are You F.A.T.

Faithful

Are you faithful to do the little things that no one else sees?

Do you show up when there is no reward in it for you?

Are you willing to stack chairs and empty trash?

Thought: If you can't be bothered to do the little things well, you are probably operating out of pride and not faithfulness.

Available

Are you okay not being in charge?

Are you willing to do what is not in your job description when asked?

Are you willing to help others on your team succeed by putting them in the forefront?

Thought: There is a lot to be said for being available for others. Putting others first helps us push our pride and ego to the side.

Teachable

Are you willing to learn from others?

Do you ask for help?

Who have you permitted to speak into your life?

Are you masking insecurities to look better in front of others?

Thought: Unteachable leaders become the lid to their ministry. If you are not willing to learn, you will lose the capacity to lead.

Chapter 3- Pride

Chapter 4- Betrayal

"Betrayal can be extremely painful, but it's up to you how much that pain damages you permanently."

-Emily V. Gordon

"When Joseph's brothers saw him coming, they recognized him in the distance. As he approached, they made plans to kill him. 19 "Here comes the dreamer!" they said. 20 "Come on, let's kill him and throw him into one of these cisterns. We can tell our father, 'A wild animal has eaten him.' Then we'll see what becomes of his dreams!" 21 But when Reuben heard of their scheme, he came to Joseph's rescue. "Let's not kill him," he said. 22 "Why should we shed any blood? Let's just throw him into this empty cistern here in the wilderness. Then he'll die without our laying a hand on him." Reuben was secretly planning to rescue Joseph and return him to his father. 23 So when Joseph arrived, his brothers ripped off the beautiful robe he was wearing. 24 Then they grabbed him and threw him into the

cistern. Now the cistern was empty; there was no water in it." Genesis 37:19-24

Joseph is sent by his fathers to check on his brothers who are tending the flocks. We know that Joseph already had a difficult relationship with his brothers. That is putting it mildly. All siblings fight. Not all siblings actually plot the other's death!

I remember fighting with my brother at times. Usually, it started out as playing and ended up with me being mad at him and starting to actually fight. On more than one occasion, he reminded me that he was seven years older than me. He would pin my arms down with his knees and tap my forehead like some demented water torture. Other times, he would put me in a wrestling hold from which I could not escape. Once I fell in front of the bathroom door, and he tried to kick me, and I moved. He put a hole in the door. What was worse was that our dad was in the bathroom at the time! But never did my brother hatch a plot to kill me.

My brother was also my protector. He could push me around, torture me as brothers do, but if anyone else laid a hand on me, I knew David would take care of it. Once, a teenager in our neighborhood was messing with me. My brother waited a day or two until a group of us were all hanging out and wrestling around. My brother tackled this kid, got on top of him, and warned him to keep his hands off. I watched with incredible joy as my tormentor left crying.

Joseph had his own issues with his brothers. He had shared his dreams with his brothers, and they hated him for it. They knew he was loved by Jacob more than they were, and it caused plenty of issues. So, when they saw an opportunity to get rid of him, they planned to kill him. But Joseph had one brother looking out for him. The oldest brother, Rueben, at least decided that there was a better way. He devised a plan to protect Joseph and to keep him alive. Unfortunately for Joseph, Rueben left, and his brothers took an opportunity to be rid of him once and for all.

When Joseph is thrown into the cistern, I wonder what thoughts went through his mind. Perhaps he felt relief that at least they didn't kill him. Perhaps he felt regret for ever sharing with his brothers his dreams. Perhaps he felt a sharp sense of betrayal.

In ministry, there are going to be times when you feel betrayed. It may be a betrayal of confidence, a betrayal of a co-worker, or of a senior leader. Betrayal is a bitter and dangerous feeling. If not dealt with, it can lead to serious issues down the road.

In a 2016 study in "Science Direct," a study was done on the effects of betrayal on those who experience it and those who perpetrate it. The stages of betrayal on those who experience it were denial, anger, bargaining, depression, and acceptance. Do those sound familiar? There are five of the six stages people go through when they experience grief. The study also shows that a person who feels betrayed goes through stages of shock and obsession. We can't believe what has happened, and it is all we can think about.

In this study, they found that those who experience betrayal have shorter leukocyte telomeres. Leukocytes are immune system cells, and telomeres are the ends of chromosomes that shorten as cells divide. The length of a person's telomeres is believed to be a possible indicator of cellular aging. Literally, betrayal causes us to age faster than normal. Betrayal acts as if it is killing us.

My friend Todd, a youth pastor in New York, had just led the most successful retreat of his ministry when, the following Tuesday, his pastor asked to see him. Expecting praise or a raise, he was instead told the elders had voted to ask for his immediate resignation—no explanation other than he "didn't fit and was too contemporary." He was given two months to move out of the church-owned home. His wife, who worked at the church's preschool, also lost her job.

What made it worse: one of the elders who voted to fire him had joined him on the retreat, praying with him nightly and praising the experience—never once hinting at what was coming.

The following year was brutal. Unable to find another ministry job, Todd worked under-the-table gigs while his family of four lived in a one-bedroom apartment. His children took turns sleeping on the floor and couch. Each morning, Todd woke up thinking, "I hate those people." Rejection piled up as churches kept turning him down—often after strong initial interviews.

Joseph probably had all the same feelings. They were well deserved. He had been betrayed by his brothers and thrown into a cistern. We skip over the time of Joseph being in the cistern, but it is a part of the story we should dive into.

As you may or may not know, a cistern is a hole in the ground designed to catch rainwater and hold it for use. Cisterns of that day were anywhere between 30-100 feet deep. Genesis 37:22 tells us that the cistern was empty. That means Joseph was thrown into the cistern and fell, at a minimum 30 feet. What happens when someone falls 30 feet or more?

EMT's are trained to understand that a fall from 10 feet or more can be fatal. Factors such as age, physical condition, and the material someone lands on all play a part in the type of injuries. A fall from 30 feet can lead to fractures, ruptured organs, lacerations and abrasions, and possible significant brain injury.

Suppose the only material at the bottom of the cistern was just the floor of the desert. If you have ever seen a sunbaked desert floor, you know it is not a place where you want to take a hard fall. Joseph would not have been in a very good state physically, mentally, or emotionally.

I understand how a fall can cause some real pain. I didn't fall from 30 or 100 feet, and I was not thrown into a cistern by my brothers. No, I fell off roller skates, the result of trying to keep a 13-year-old middle school student from falling. In hindsight, I should have just let her fall. 13-year-olds handle falls better than 40-somethings.

When I tumbled to the ground, I didn't think much of it. Then I tried to stand. Immediately, I knew something was wrong. I could not put any weight on my left ankle. And when I looked down, my foot was pointing in, let's say, an unnatural direction. I had broken two bones in my leg and dislocated my left ankle.

That led to an ambulance trip to the ER. In the emergency room, a doctor told me they needed to reset my ankle, and I was not going to want to be awake for this part. I had surgery, and two plates and three screw were inserted into my ankle and leg. For twelve weeks, I could not put any weight on my leg. And after the twelve weeks came months of physical therapy. Eight years later, I had the hardware removed from my leg and have a huge scar to help tell this story.

I wonder as I read the story of Joseph, what physical wounds he had from the fall? Did he break a bone? Did he have cuts all over his body? Did he have to limp as he walked through the desert to Egypt. Did the scars last?

We don't know the answer to those questions. But I know there were scars. They may not have been physical. They may not be obvious. But you can't be betrayed as Joseph was and not have scars.

> *"Judah said to his brothers, "What will we gain by killing our brother? We'd have to cover up the crime. 27 Instead of hurting him, let's sell him to those Ishmaelite traders. After all, he is our brother—our own flesh and blood!" And his brothers agreed. 28 So when the Ishmaelites, who were Midianite traders, came by, Joseph's brothers pulled him out of the cistern and sold him to them for twenty pieces of silver. And the traders took him to Egypt."*
> *Genesis 37:26-28*

Joseph was not only betrayed by being thrown into a cistern, but he was also sold for twenty pieces of silver. This is actually a very low price for a young man of Joseph's age and physical ability. It shows his brother's disdain for him and that they simply wanted him to be gone.

When we find ourselves dealing with betrayal as Joseph or Todd did, it is easy for us to lose sight of anything else. It is hard to see that a great turning point is around the corner. It is hard to believe that we are going to come out of the darkness. Most of the time, in seasons of betrayal, we feel as if even God has abandoned us.

One Sunday, my friend Todd reluctantly visited a church that met in a theater. During worship, a video sermon began: "Today we are finishing our study on the life of Job." As the pastor said, "Some of you are in a dark season, and God wants you to know you're about to come out of it." Todd felt as if God was speaking directly to him. His wife was in tears.

The next morning, Todd woke up for the first time in months without bitterness. Healing had begun.

Soon after, he got a call from a church in Ohio— "a church for broken people." Despite poor feedback from his previous church, they felt Todd was the right fit. He accepted the position, and God provided a home that perfectly met their needs.

The betrayal was real, and the impact was raw and painful. No one goes through those seasons without scars. They may be physical, emotional, or spiritual. But they don't have to be fatal. They can lead us to healing and to healthy ministry again.

There is a singular verse in the story of Joseph that we must never overlook or skim over. It is as true for us today as it was for Joseph.

> *"The Lord was with Joseph..."*
> *Genesis 39:2*

Through all of Joseph's pain and difficulties, God had not abandoned him. And through all our pain and seasons of betrayal, God has not left us alone. As you walk through the dark nights and listless days, remember the truth that you are not alone. God has never and will never abandon you in your betrayal.

Hold Fast

In John 13, Jesus washes the feet of the disciples, including Judas. What lessons can that teach us about dealing with those who have betrayed us?

Stay True

How Are You Dealing with Betrayal

Walk through the questions below with a sheet of paper and do an honest assessment.

Who

Who has betrayed you?

What was the situation?

Do you make excuses for the other party's actions?

Thought: Being honest about who betrayed you is a critical step in dealing with the hurt. Write out the situation as best as you can remember to bring it clearly to mind.

Affect

How has it affected you mentally and emotionally?

How has it impacted you spiritually?

How has it touched your family?

Does this betrayal cause you to lack trust in others?

Thought: We can't heal from the effects of an illness unless we identify the hurts. Be honest about the pain

God

How has your pain impacted your relationship with God?

Who has God placed in your life, whom you can trust, to walk alongside you?

Have you given up your faith because of the betrayal of a certain person?

Thought: Do the hard work of the soul. Be honest with God about the condition of your heart.

Chapter 5-Exile

"Exile is not a time frame. Exile is an experience. It's a sentiment." Marco Rubio

Joseph had been betrayed by his brothers, almost killed, thrown into a deep pit, taken out of the pit, and sold into slavery. That was a horrible, terrible, no good, very bad day! Joseph probably came out of the pit injured, confused, frustrated, and scared. Now, not only was he experiencing these emotions, but he was also being sent off with a band of traders. Joseph had been sold into slavery and was exiled from his own country.

> *"So, when the Ishmaelites, who were Midianite traders, came by, Joseph's brothers pulled him out of the cistern and sold him to them for twenty pieces of silver. And the traders took him to Egypt."* Genesis 37:28

Joseph had not only been sold as a slave, but then he was taken to a country he had never seen, to a culture he didn't know, into a land where he didn't know the language. Joseph had, in the course of one day, been betrayed, sold, and exiled.

When we think of exile in our modern sense, we think of political leaders who have been removed from power and sent to live in a foreign country or groups of people moved from one nation to the next during war. Our minds may think of Napoleon, exiled from France to the Isle of Elba. We have learned in history about the millions of Jews displaced in World War II. Or perhaps you remember or have heard of the Shah of Iran in the 1970s, who was overthrown and came to live in the United States.

But being in exile is not reserved for those persecuted groups or deposed leaders. Exile can also be of an individual or a family, and it may be a voluntary decision. People leave one country for another in search of a new life, a new job, or a better future for their children. In ministry, it is not uncommon for us to self-exile for some of those same reasons.

The average pastor serves at their church for four years. For that statistic to be true, think of all the pastors who have been at their church for longer than four years. They have built a legacy. Now you must also realize that for the statistic to be true, think of all the pastors who have not stayed at their church for four years. That number is alarming. And among non-senior pastor staff positions, the average length of time at a local ministry is around three years.

In other words, being a person in full-time ministry means that at some point, you are going to leave one position and begin another. And when we leave churches, we never expect that we are going to find ourselves in exile. We assume we are going to find a legitimate community, encouraging support, and a home for the rest of our lives. We rarely change positions from one ministry to another, assuming we will only last about three years.

My ministry journey has taken me to serve at four local churches, one international mission, and one faith-based non-profit. I served at my first church for 9 years, my second for four, my third for ten and a half years, our international non-profit for three years, an associate position for a church for three years before it closed. I have been in my present position for eight years so far. Only one time did I think the position I was in was going to be short-term. When I began to serve the mission in Haiti, I knew it was not a long-term ministry, but a place for me to invest in others for a season.

While I have served several ministries over my 36 years in ministry, I have only had one major move. After 9 years as the student pastor in California, my family and I relocated to South Florida. Honestly, when we were being pursued by the church in Florida, we were not interested. We resisted calls and had determined that we were exactly where we needed to be. But after many weeks of prayer and resistance, Alana and I knew we had to at least listen to the offer.

When we arrived in South Florida, it was like being in a different country. Apart from about three years when she was a little girl, my wife had never lived outside of California. I grew up in Tennessee but had spent 13 years in California. When we stepped off the plane in September, we were greeted with two things we were unprepared for...humidity and green. My wife had grown up in the desert of California. All the landscaping in her world was brown and consisted of rocks. I had grown up in Tennessee, but the weight of the air in South Florida was not what I had experienced.

The church we were headed to was a traditional Southern Baptist church. Alana and I had both grown up in the Southern Baptist tradition, so we understood it a little bit. But I had never served at a traditional church before. We quickly learned that we were in a new place, with a new culture, and even a new language we didn't fully grasp.

In California, our ministry was grounded in evangelism and discipleship and grew through hard work invested at local public-school campuses. In Florida, I was expected to be in the office for hours upon hours each day, and the largest ministry for students that was occurring was a youth choir. That was uncharted territory! In California, our culture was relaxed and informal. In Florida, I was expected to wear dress pants to the office and a suit and tie on Sundays. In California, everyone called our pastor by his first name. In Florida, it was expected that you would call the pastor, Pastor.

I also learned that some of the things I had been told about the church when I was interviewing were not necessarily correct. I was told that the church was averaging about 1,000 people on Sundays. In reality, it had 1,000 members on roll and about 600 on Sundays. I was new to the idea of membership rolls. I was used to a dynamic in leadership of shared value, consensus decision making, and a friendship with my senior pastor. While I was told those things were valued, I learned quickly that I was a part of a hierarchy I had never experienced before.

But Alana and I were certain that God had called us here. So, we dug in, began to learn the culture and the language, and did our best to carry out the ministry we were called to oversee. We created discipleship models. We began to engage in youth choir and develop student leaders based on the depth of their spiritual life, and not their grade or popularity. And it created waves. During that first year, I could feel the contempt from some of the upperclassmen and their parents. But I was convinced that if they would just buy in, we would see God move. And we did. Some of those seniors just complained and killed time until they graduated. But others loved the new focus.

By our second year, the tide was turning. We were seeing new students show up, students sharing the gospel with their friends, and a surge in our discipleship model. But at the same time, there were deep undercurrents of unhealth. I had begun to see some patterns of behavior in leadership that were unsettling. There was not an even flow of decision-making and idea sharing. Instead, I found myself in an autocratic model that I didn't understand.

I remember coming home from a staff retreat late one night, about six to eight months into our time there. Alana and the kids were already in bed, so I tried to slide into bed as quietly as possible. Apparently, I let out a sigh, because Alana turned over and said, "What's the matter?" That's when I broke down for the first time.

I remember telling her that I thought we had made a huge mistake. We had left a ministry and people we loved, uprooted our family, and moved literally across the country, and I felt like we were in the wrong place. I remember the unsettled feeling I had as I tried to wrestle with what had happened at the retreat. I don't remember anything crazy or outrageous; I just knew things did not sit well in my heart.

I had never experienced anything like this. Over the next couple of years, I watched repeatedly as people left our church. I watched as decisions were made, not for what was best for the ministry, but what would look best to the community around us. I saw how finances were manipulated, how numbers were bulked up to look good on reports, and how Godly people were dismissed from ministry if they asked the wrong questions.

Amid all of this, I focused on the students and watched as God did some incredible ministry. While chaos seemed to swirl around us, God was faithfully leading students to himself, and students were growing in their depth and maturity in Christ.

I also made some huge mistakes. I expressed my frustrations to other staff far too often. Although they shared my concerns, I should not have been so open with my feelings. I was also too honest when asked questions by leadership. I had been in a culture where, when your opinion was wanted, you were expected to give it honestly. That was not the culture here. I offered on more than one occasion to resign and seek another position but was told to wait to resign until another position came. That was another two years!!!

During that time, two things sustained us. First, we had some great relationships with other adults who loved our family and walked through some difficult times with us. We were blessed beyond belief. One time, our septic system had issues, and it was going to be way more expensive to fix than we could afford. A check arrived at our doorstep. On another occasion, my ten-year-old car had irreparable engine problems. A friend's mother had gotten a new car and gave us a Volvo that we drove the wheels off!

The second thing that sustained us was the growth we were seeing in the students. We were seeing new students show up at the ministry who had been invited by friends. We were seeing lives given to Christ. We even saw that youth choir record an album because someone donated funds to have it produced. God was still working in the midst of our exile.

> *"When Joseph was taken to Egypt by the Ishmaelite traders, he was purchased by Potiphar, an Egyptian officer. Potiphar was captain of the guard for Pharaoh, the king of Egypt. ² The Lord was with Joseph, so he succeeded in everything he did as he served in the home of his Egyptian master.: Genesis 39:1-2*

Joseph did all he could, faithfully serving his master. God was with Joseph, and he succeeded in all his jobs. The lesson I learn from these verses is that when we are in exile, we still must do all we can to honor God in our work. I am reminded of the words Paul wrote to the Corinthians:

> *"So whether you eat or drink, or whatever you do, do it all for the glory of God."*
> *1 Corinthians 10:31*

What I also learned in this season was that if we are faithful to what God has called us to, we can trust him to guide our steps. Students from our ministry have become pastors, missionaries, and worship pastors. They have also become faithful, Godly businessmen and women, teachers, and Godly parents. That is not because of who I was in their lives, but because of who God is. When we live out our genuine selves in front of others, they begin to see God in us.

If you find yourself in a season of exile, you have some choices to make. You can leave and find another job to support your family. And that is a valid thing to do. You can stay and serve where you are, but learn how to honor your leaders as best you can. Or you can stand and fight. You can become the source of division or become the spark of unity. There are so many things I wish I had done differently. But I did learn through this season.

You may feel like you are in exile, but here are some truths to hang onto.

God has not abandoned you.

God did not abandon Joseph, and he will not abandon you. He was with Joseph in the pit, in the caravan to Egypt, and in the service of Potipher.

Serve as if you will be there the rest of your life.

We have no idea of God's timetable for us. We have plans and purposes for our lives, but God has more in store for us than we could ever imagine.

Honor those who oversee you.

I honestly did not do a great job in this area. But Joseph did. When Potiphar's wife tried to seduce him, which we will look at in more detail in the next chapter, he would not betray Potiphar or God for temporary pleasure.

Speak honestly and honorably to those and about those in charge.

Determine your non-negotiables and resign when you can no longer honestly live those out in your ministry.

As we learn from Joseph, exile is temporary in the Kingdom of God. Even if we are never delivered from it on this side of heaven, we know that our eternal home is being prepared for us by Jesus right now. The best we can do right now is to do the best we can in service of Jesus. Stay faithful, stay connected to Christ and serve faithfully where God has planted you in this season.

Hold Fast

Read Psalm 147:1-3 What does this passage teach us about exiles?

Stay True

Here are some thoughts to think about as you minister in Exile:

How did you get here?

Did you move from one place to another, thinking it would be better?

What was it you wanted to change?

Were you not told the truth of the culture you were stepping into?

Thought: Understanding how we got here is the key to making sure we never end up here again. If we are always looking for the next best place, the flashier toys, or the bigger salary, we may find ourselves heading to a place we won't see as home.

What has this season done to your walk with Christ?

Are you blaming God for where you are?

Did you take baggage from one ministry assignment to another?

Do you feel as if God has abandoned you?

Do you feel as if you have let God down?

Thought: We are never told that Joseph ever heard from God. We are simply told that God was with Joseph. The same God with Joseph is the same God who is present with you.

What are your next steps?

Is it time to go?

Do you need to step out of your comfort zone to get out of exile?

Do you need to live in a new culture?

Who can you confidently and confidentially discuss this season with?

Thought: Don't walk through this season alone. Share it with your spouse but also find trusted people you can be open and honest with who will give you Godly, biblical counsel from someone outside your ministry context.

Chapter 6 - Temptation

"I can resist everything except temptation."
- Oscar Wilde

What's your thing? What's the thing in your life that you can never say no to if it is offered to you? I love coffee. I will drink about five cups before noon. I love it and when I don't get to have all the coffee I want, it makes me a little cranky. No, you are not the first person to point out my addiction. My wife loves tacos. If you ask her, would she rather have tacos or BBQ for dinner, ten out of ten times the answer is tacos! Alana is an elementary school teacher. One day, as she walked her class back from lunch, a little boy asked her what she had for lunch. By chance, she had brought leftover tacos from home. When she replied, "Tacos," the little guy shouted, "You love tacos!!" Out of the mouths of babes!

We all have the things we love and the delicacies we won't give up. I have had people repeatedly, through the years, tell me to give up coffee. But it will never happen. I once fasted from coffee for 30 days. Alana begged me never to do that again! Coffee and tacos may be harmless enough. Please don't send me emails or scientific studies. But what happens when the tantalizing thing leads us on a more dangerous path?

I love C.S. Lewis. Last year, Alana and I were able to visit Oxford, England, and see where he taught. One of the highlights was visiting The Kilns, Lewis's home outside of Oxford. Today, it is a nice, cozy little community in the English countryside. But when Lewis was there, it was surrounded by woods and ponds.

On the side of his house is a little staircase that ascends to his bedroom. On that staircase, he would look out onto the woods, Narnia if you will, and write "The Chronicles of Narnia." I love those books. I can't recall how often I have read them. But my favorite, to this day, is still "The Lion, the Witch, and the Wardrobe." I love the imagery, the introduction of Aslan, and the Deep Magic. The image of a Christ-figure as a lion has always fascinated me. I know scripture tells us Jesus is the Lion of Judah, but picturing Aslan prowling around Cair Paravel and crowning kings and queens ignites my soul.

But before they could be crowned, they had to deal with the temptation of Turkish Delight. Do you remember how the White Witch got Edmund to first experience Turkish Delight? It seemed like a harmless treat to be had with a warm drink. In reality, it was creating a thirst and a craving for more that could never be satisfied. And it was leading Edmund to a path of destruction he couldn't see.

That is how temptation works. It seems harmless enough. It seems like there is no danger, especially if no one finds out. And sometimes, we actually believe we are immune to temptation.

As we pick up the story of Joseph, we find that God has blessed him as he has served in the house of Potiphar. The scripture tells us:

> *"Potiphar noticed this and realized that the Lord was with Joseph, giving him success in everything he did. 4 This pleased Potiphar, so he soon made Joseph his personal attendant. He put him in charge of his entire household and everything he owned." Genesis 39:3-4*

Joseph was blessed by God to succeed in all he did and was rewarded by his master by being placed over all the affairs of the house. We find in scripture that Joseph was a very handsome and well-built young man. And Potiphar's wife noticed. She begged him to come in and sleep with her. And Joseph could have arranged to get away with it. After all, he could have orchestrated to be alone in the house whenever he wanted. And day after day, she tried to entice Joseph. And day after day, Joseph refused.

Joseph tried to plead with her by arguing that it would be a wicked thing to do to his master. But day after day, she kept after him. Joseph tried to appeal to her on his religious grounds. But day after day, she kept after him.

One of the dangers of ministry is that temptation of one kind or another is always around. Nothing has changed from the earliest days of scripture to modern day. And sex is just one of the incredible temptations. Sex, money, power, fame, and the lust for more is a lethal mixture for people in ministry. Even more dangerous is that so often people don't see the danger until it is too late. I literally had a man in ministry tell me he was immune to temptation because he was a "Man of God." He could not have been more wrong. The truth is, we all face temptations. How we respond to them makes all the difference in the world.

Part of what made Joseph the man he was is the very fact that, although he did not have written scripture, did not have the Holy Spirit dwelling inside him; he relied on the stories of the faithfulness of God to guide him in every situation. The fact that God was with him and that he succeeded in all that he did points us to the unwritten declaration, "because he obeyed God."

Success in ministry is not a sign of spiritual obedience or the absence of sin. So many stories of pastors who led thriving, growing, disciple-making ministries have led to the uncovering of some very dark, very hidden sin issues. We could create a long list of people who fit that model. An even longer list would be of people whose names we do not know, whose ministries are small and unseen, and who have served faithfully in anonymity for years. But deep in the background is hidden, unconfessed sin.

No one ever heads down a road of hidden sin knowingly. No one ever plans an addiction, an affair, or a financial sin. Everyone gets into ministry because they feel a call from God, they desire to serve, and they have a heart for others. But when obedience gets pushed aside by temptation, sin takes root.

In our modern culture it may not be a woman on a bed enticing us to sleep with her. But what about the images on your phone? What about the videos on your computer? How do we deal with what we see every day in our culture?

Scripture is crystal clear about how to prepare daily for the spiritual battles we will face. Ephesians 6 tells us to put on the armor of God. James tells us to "resist the devil." James 4:7. In other words, we prepare for a fight, and we fight. But there is one instance where we are told not to stand and fight.

"Run from sexual sin!" 1 Corinthians 6:18

When it comes to sexual sin, we are not told to stand as in Ephesians 6 or resist as in James 4. We are told to run! Why is it that we are told to take such drastic actions? I believe it is because God knows the human heart and that we are only capable of being formidable so long. God created us as sexual beings, but we are to confine our sexuality to his standard of one man and one woman in a covenant marriage relationship.

But our culture blasts away at this idea. We are force-fed an endless display of sex to sell products, convince us to buy certain cars, and to buy body sprays that drive the women wild. Middle school boys believe a can of Axe and an ounce of confidence beats out a good shower and witty banter!

As people in ministry, the dangers of not protecting ourselves as God tells us in scripture is like ignoring warning signs of dangerous surf. Where I live in Florida, the beach is one of the most popular destinations for tourists and locals. But every beach has a sign that tells you the water temperature, the presence of sea life, and the surf conditions. Far too often, people ignore the warning signs of an undercurrent and find themselves fighting for their lives to reach shore. Last year, a friend of mine from high school drowned because she was trying to help someone caught in a rip current. Two months ago, on his last day of high school, a graduating senior died because he ignored the signs that warned of the danger.

In ministry, we are not only dealing with organizations, visions, and plans, but ultimately, we are ministering to people. Often, the people we are meeting with are hurting, feeling betrayed, and dealing with issues that impact the heart. This leads to misplaced feelings, distorted views of intimacy, and makes them and us vulnerable to giving in to temptation. Without very strict guidelines and strategies, the most well-meaning pastor can find himself in dangerous waters.

When temptations arise, we need to look to Joseph. Look at Joseph's response after day after day of Potiphar's wife tempting him.

> *"One day, however, no one else was around when he went in to do his work.* **12** *She came and grabbed him by his cloak, demanding, "Come on, sleep with me!" Joseph tore himself away, but he left his cloak in her hand as he ran from the house. Genesis 39:11-12*

Joseph didn't have a lot of options for doing his work. Remember, he is a slave. But when he went in on this particular day, the house was empty. As usual, Potiphar's wife made her plea for Joseph to sin against her husband and against God. Notice that Joseph didn't try to stand and reason with her. He didn't weigh his options. He didn't balance out the pros and cons. Joseph tore himself away and ran.

The problem we have in dealing with temptation is that far too often, we don't want to tear ourselves away and run!! We try to reason our way around it. "Is it that big of a deal if I look at that website?" "The church won't miss this small amount of money I spend on myself out of my expense account." "Everyone else is watching 'Game of Thrones' why shouldn't I?" Small compromises lead to disastrous results.

When the White Witch offered a warm drink and a snack to Edmund, he never thought it would create a craving. He never assumed where it would lead. The first pastor I ever worked for, Bill Walthall, said the problem most men deal with is not that they fantasize too much, but that they don't fantasize far enough. What he meant was that when faced with temptation, we only go as far as the thrill of fulfilling that desire. And sin, by its nature, is pleasurable for a moment or else it wouldn't be tempting. Bill argued that men don't carry the fantasy to completion. Completion is not when the act is over. Completion is the guilt and shame we feel before God. Completion is having to confess to our spouse and children what we have done. Sometimes, completion is losing your family, your ministry, your reputation, your house, and your savings. If we ever allowed ourselves to see that far down the road, it would probably lead more of us to run from temptation like Joseph.

Sin has a high cost. When Aslan pays for the sins of Edmund on the Stone Table, all of Narnia is shaken. Of course, this is an allegory of Jesus on the cross. When Jesus died on the cross, the world literally went dark. And every sin you would ever have committed was placed on the shoulders of Jesus.

Because our sins have been paid for, we must focus our minds, not on the things of this world, but on the things of God. Paul tells us in Romans,

"But you are not controlled by your sinful nature. You are controlled by the Spirit if you have the Spirit of God living in you."
Romans 8:9

Temptation begins in the mind. If we do not have a mind transformed by God, we are living at the edge of sin. Sin begins in the mind, travels to the heart, and reveals itself in our actions. Temptation is a mind game first.

Where does temptation show up in your life? If you are anything like me, there is an ironic twist to temptation. Most of the time in my ministry, temptation has arisen after a huge ministry win. I speak at a camp where God moves in powerful ways. When I get home on that Saturday night, I can guarantee you that something is going to come across the television screen that is going to lead me into temptation.

When I am tired after a week on a mission trip, as I travel home, there will be a movie or a magazine that catches my eye. Alone in a hotel at a conference is a time when we are vulnerable and can easily become trapped in temptations.

I have a friend who is a pilot. He travels the world and has all kinds of incredible adventures. He travels so much that at times I have called him while he was on the road and asked where he was and he had to check the information in his hotel room to remember what city he is in! He usually is away from home for seven or eight nights per trip. That means seven or eight nights away from his wife and kids. Seven or eight nights away from his church community. He is on the road and could do anything he wants, and there is a good chance no one would know.

My friend has developed a strategy to help him avoid compromise in his walk with Christ. First, he places a picture of his family near the television in his room. This reminds him of what is at stake if he makes poor decisions. Second, he takes his bible and Christian books with him. This feeds his mind spiritual food. Finally, he has a direct line to call me at any time. If he finds himself in a situation, he doesn't feel comfortable in, he picks up the phone and reaches out to a Christian brother.

If we don't take practical, real steps to guard against temptation, we will put ourselves in circumstances where we risk everything. With access to anything and everything in our pockets, protecting ourselves from ourselves is more important than ever. If you do not have a device monitoring system with accountability to another Christian on your computer, iPad, and phone, you are putting yourself in a place of temptation. I have a system set up on my phone that sends a report every week to my wife of any website I have visited. I get a report every day from a friend of mine of all his electronic browsing. You may think that is childish, immature, or that you are beyond the need, but these systems, while not foolproof, add a layer of accountability to my life. And I know I need it.

But what if you have already blown it? Maybe you haven't had a full-fledged affair, but you are struggling with pornography, or you have allowed alcohol to have a hold on you, or you have fudged on your finances one too many times? Are you completely counted out? Are you disqualified? Are you beyond hope?

The most direct answer is NO! Your failures are not final, and they are rarely fatal. While there may need to be some time for confession, repentance, healing, and restoration, you are not a lost soul. When. Christ died for your sins; he died for all your sins. And when you became his child, you were adopted into a family that will be yours for eternity. Your relationship with Christ may be distant, but it is never over. So, how do we deal with our failure?

Confess. You already know this, but the first act of coming back to a right relationship with God is confession. We sometimes wrongly think that confession is giving God new information. God knows all about your sin. Confession is agreeing with God that we have sinned against him. The first relationship we must restore is the relationship with our Heavenly Father.

After confessing to God, we need to confess to our spouse. It is not enough just to have a sidebar with God and assume everything is fine. It is only when we can have an honest confession with our spouse that we can begin to heal the deep wounds that our sin has caused. Be strategic, be honest, be sensitive, and be vulnerable.

Repent. Repentance is not the same as confession. As you know, repentance is a change of direction from sin to God. It is when we begin to change our minds, our words, our actions daily that we begin to see the fruit of repentance. Repentance is a daily decision. It is a choice to live as obedient sons and daughters. Repentance leads us to sanctification.

Get Help. Don't try to walk through all of these issues alone. There are some incredible ministries that serve people in ministry who are dealing with every issue in this book. Standing Stone, Care for Pastors, and other faithful ministries can help you and your family heal from all kinds of emotional, spiritual, mental, and sinful issues.

What about my ministry? That is always a leading question. If I confess my struggles, am I going to lose my job? Will others see me as a failure? How will I provide for my family? All of these questions are very real and very scary. And I can't answer them. I have seen and experienced in my own life churches that have walked through painful issues with incredible compassion and tender grace. I have also seen people come forward and confess sin and be met with judgment and a severance check.

What I can tell you is this: being free from your sin, operating with a clean slate, loving and caring for your family, and serving in ministry at whatever capacity you are allowed is far greater than the stability of your job. You may have all kinds of fears and doubts, but remember, those grow in the dark. Right standing with God, with your family, your ministry, and yourself brings you into the incredible light of grace.

After Edmund's failure with the White Witch, after the sacrifice of Aslan on the Stone Table, and after Aslan's triumphant return, Aslan, Peter, Susan, Edmund, and Lucy are all at Cair Paravel. Aslan, strong as a lion and regal as a king, crowns all four of the children as kings and queens. Their debt has been paid, their sin forgiven, and their future secured. In the midst of the celebration, Aslan speaks these words,

"Once a king or queen of Narnia, always a king or queen. Bear it well, Sons of Adam! Bear it well, Daughters of Eve!"

You have been crowned with an eternal crown by our Heavenly Father based on the sacrifice and resurrection of Jesus. You didn't earn it, and you cannot lose it. Your failures are not final, and they are very rarely fatal. So, continue to live as a son or daughter of the King!

Hold Fast

Read 1 Corinthians 10:13. What is the promise of God in dealing with our temptations?

Stay True

Dealing with your temptation.

What is your temptation?

What would be the outcome if you gave in to that temptation?

Thought: Identifying and playing out the end result of your temptation is the beginning step to overcoming.

What triggers your temptation?

Is it tiredness?

Do you struggle after a ministry win?

Are you more aware of your temptation when you are alone?

Knowing what triggers us helps us develop strategies to avoid temptations.

What do you need to confess?

Get it all out in the open.

Who do you need to confess to?

Get some help.

We don't overcome by hiding our sin in the dark.

Seek help from trusted and safe ministry leaders.

Be ready to deal with the consequences of sin.

Chapter 7- Prison

"No, my dear Dantes. I know perfectly well that you are innocent. Why else would you be here? If you were truly guilty, there are a hundred prisons in France where they would lock you away. But Chateau d'If is where is they put the ones they're ashamed of."

Dorleac in "The Count of Monte Cristo"

One of my family's favorite movies is "The Count of Monte Cristo." It is a classic piece of literature, but the 2002 movie starring Jim Caviezel and Guy Pearce is an incredible telling of the story. Set in France between 1815 and 1839, the story centers around the relationship between Edmond Dantes and Fernond de Moncerf. While Dantes comes from a poor family, he becomes friends with Moncerf, who comes from a wealthy, aristocratic background.

As most of these stories go, there a beautiful woman, Mercedes, who loves Edmond, but is desired by Fernond. For Fernond to have his chance with Mercedes, he must get rid of Edmond. And so, he does. He sets up a scenario where Edmond is arrested and falsely accused of treason because of a chance meeting with Napoleon on Malta. (You really need to watch this movie!!!)

Basically, Edmond gets sent to a notoriously dark and deadly prison from which no one has left alive or escaped. Well, of course....no, you really need to see for yourself. For our purposes, I wanted to use this story to help us set up the story of Joseph, wrongly sent to prison.

When Potiphar's wife does not get her way with Joseph, she makes up a lie that he tried to rape her. Because Joseph ran away and left his coat, it is assumed by Potiphar that the story is true. Honestly, Joseph's life would have been much easier if he stopped wearing a coat! Here is where we pick up the biblical account...

> *"Potiphar was furious when he heard his wife's story about how Joseph had treated her. 20 So he took Joseph and threw him into the prison where the king's prisoners were held, and there he remained."* *Genesis 39:19-20*

Joseph remained in prison for at least two years. He is falsely accused, wrongly arrested, and unjustly sentenced. Amazing how Joseph's life foreshadows the life of Jesus in this way. But again, we find that while he was in prison, God was with Joseph.

"But the Lord was with Joseph in the prison and showed him his faithful love."
Genesis 39:21

The Hebrew word from which we get the word "With" is the Hebrew word *ayth*. When this word is used in this context, it means nearness or closeness. What a great image to have. That God is close to you, even in prison. Not only that, but God also demonstrated his faithful love, *hesed* in the Hebrew. This is an intimate, unfailing love. It is the type of love we refer to in the New Testament Greek as *agape*.

Joseph again finds himself in a place he never dreamed of, in circumstances beyond his control, and dealing with attacks on his character. But Joseph did what he always did in that scenario: he worked with excellence.

"And the Lord made Joseph a favorite with the prison warden. 22 Before long, the warden put Joseph in charge of all the other prisoners and over everything that happened in the prison. 23 The warden had no more worries because Joseph took care of everything. The Lord was with him and caused everything he did to succeed."
Genesis 39:21-23

I pray that we never find ourselves in an actual prison. But at times, what happens to Joseph in prison may seem like our circumstances. In ministry, you will find yourself, at times, in a place you never dreamed of, in circumstances beyond your control, and with people attacking your character.

I have dealt with those issues before. After 10 and a half years as a Lead Pastor, my wife and I both felt like our time was up serving that church. We had poured our hearts and souls into creating the needed transition. We have grown from a dying church of 20 people to a church running close to 150 people. It doesn't sound like a huge victory, but God had held this group together through some major growing pains. If you skipped the introduction of this book, I encourage you to go back and read it for context.

The church was struggling financially. We had a mortgage we were barely able to pay, and it was harder for the church to maintain a full-time pastor. I approached our elders about becoming bi-vocational. I had developed a strong tie to the mission in Haiti that I eventually served with, and they needed some pastoral help. I had run this idea by some very close friends in ministry, and they all believed it was a solid plan.

When I approached the elders with a detailed plan, they were less than enthusiastic. After a week of discussion among themselves, I was asked to meet with them to discuss the plan. Expecting to hear that they had decided to take my advice, instead, I was met with a letter telling me I had no integrity, and they were disappointed that I had even suggested the plan. After a long discussion, I submitted my resignation.

Chapter 7- Prison

We established a timeline of a month that I would wrap up my ministry, and then I would move on.

These were men I had spent over a decade of my life serving alongside. We had been in each other's homes, and we had vacationed together. And now, they were not only not pleased with my plan, but they also questioned my character. I served one more month and was shown the door. I wasn't paid for my last month. My severance package was that I got to keep my seven-year-old computer.

There are times when your circumstances are not what you imagined. But that does not mean God is not nearby. My wife was a stay-at-home mom during this time. She had been the children's director for $500 a month at our church, but the past year, that position was eliminated. She continued to serve in that role, just as a volunteer. This was most assuredly not our plan.

Just this past week, Alana and I were discussing this season of our lives. We have no idea how we paid our bills. We have no idea how we fed the kids, and we have no idea exactly how it all came together. Except that our God was near.

When you find yourself in places and circumstances outside of your control, the nearness of God may be all you can rely on. When you don't know where the money will come from, you can trust that God is with you. It sounds like a cliché, but God has told us in his word,

"Don't love money; be satisfied with what you have. For God has said, "I will never fail you. I will never abandon you." Hebrews 13:5

As human beings, we naturally worry and stress, especially over finances. Money can become an incredibly large focus of stress and division that can lead to the breakdown of the family. But God has called us to a different level of understanding. We must press in toward him. We must trust that he is nearby. We must determine that what others do and say toward us is not the final word.

While Joseph was in prison, God was near, and he blessed Joseph with success. Joseph also had a flashback of dealing with dreams. While he is in prison, he interprets dreams for the baker and the cupbearer of Pharaoh. They had both offended Pharaoh and were now paying the price. Scholars believe that perhaps there had been a plot to murder Pharaoh, and these men were suspects.

It was good news for the cupbearer. In three days, Pharaoh was going to restore him to his former job. The baker, well, his dream did not have such a happy ending. The baker was going to be executed in three days. Joseph interpreted their dreams, with the help of God, and asked that the cupbearer remember Joseph when he is restored to his position. He agreed to this, but scripture tells us...

Chapter 7- Prison

"Pharaoh's chief cupbearer, however, forgot all about Joseph, never giving him another thought." Genesis 40:23

Joseph was forgotten and still in prison. Sometimes in our ministry, we may feel as though we are forgotten. We put our heads down, we serve faithfully, and we never get the credit, the raise, the promotion, or the respect we deserve. Instead of being rewarded for faithfulness, it feels like we are not only pushed to the side, but we are pushed out of mind.

When this happens, we have two options. We can go to our corner, sulk in our emotions, and complain about how unfair life is. Or we can do what Joseph did for a full two years, faithfully serve where we are and trust that God sees our faithfulness. Joseph went about his daily duties in the prison, and God saw his work. He excelled and made a great reputation for himself. But he was still in prison.

Sometimes, it seems like the goal of ministry is recognition. We want people to tell us what a great job we are doing. We dream of some students referencing our influence in a graduation speech. In our modern culture, the ultimate sign we have made it is that we have a platform!

While all those things are wonderful and they feed the ego, they should never be the goal. Instead, we should have a goal that leads others to Jesus, shows them what it means to live for him, and encourages them to help others do the same.

We started this chapter with the story of The Count of Monte Cristo. We will wrap up his story a little later, but I want to point you to the story of another Count.

Nicklaus Ludwig von Zizendorf was born into one of the most prominent and wealthy families of Germany in 1700. He became a deep religious scholar and was moved with compassion for those in suffering. He vehemently opposed slavery and worked with missionaries to minister to those impacted by slavery. Count Zizendorf rose to become a man who provided protection and shelter for Moravian missionaries who were being threatened by slave owners.

When Zizendorf was a bishop in the Moravian Church, he once said that his role was to "preach the gospel, die, and be forgotten." It's ironic that a man who preached about being forgotten is being discussed several hundred years after his death. But it seems to me that our role in ministry is not our recognition, our fame, or our platform. It is the name, recognition, and platform of Jesus we should desire.

While Joseph may have been forgotten by the cupbearer in prison for a season, ultimately God brought him to mind and positioned him to be not only restored, but elevated.

Pharaoh had a dream that deeply disturbed him. He could not understand it, and none of his counselors could interpret it for him. It is at this moment that the cupbearer remembers his "failure" to remember

Joseph and tells Pharaoh of a prisoner who can interpret his dream.

Joseph is brought from prison, cleaned up, and finds himself before the ruler of Egypt. Pharaoh tells Joseph that he has been told Joseph can interpret dreams. But Joseph, instead of seeking credit or looking out for his own interests, gives him an unexpected reply.

> *"It is beyond my power to do this," Joseph replied. "But God can tell you what it means and set you at ease." Genesis 41:16*

Remember who Joseph is talking to. He is addressing the ruler of the nation to whom he has been sold as a slave. He is addressing a man who is considered a god by his own people. But now, he is speaking about a God that this Pharaoh doesn't believe in or acknowledge.

That should be our default response. It is not about us. Our name, our fame, and our reputation are so far secondary to the power and name and fame of God that it should never cross our minds to promote ourselves.

Yes, it is hard when we are taken for granted. Yes, it is painful and lonely to feel like we have been pushed aside and forgotten. But as "new creations in Christ," as 2 Corinthians 5:17 tells us, our old life is gone, and a new one has begun. And that new life is found in the identity as a child of God.

Edmond Dantes created a new life for himself. He entered the prison as a simple, poor sailor, and over time, he developed himself into The Count of Monte Cristo. What we see in Joseph is that he was the same person in prison that he was in the previous years of his life.

Joseph was 17 years old when he was sold into slavery by his brothers. He worked in Potiphar's house for 11 years and then spent at least two years in prison. Two phrases are repeatedly used to describe Joseph in this season: God was with Joseph, and he succeeded in everything he did.

One amazing aspect about the story of Joseph in scripture is that we are never told that God showed up to him personally and told him what was happening, and that it would all end well. Joseph never had an angel visit him like his namesake; Joseph did when Mary was pregnant. Joseph also never possessed written scripture or the indwelling Holy Spirit.

Joseph simply trusted what he had learned about God and faithfully did the work in front of him. That should be the call on all our lives. While we may feel imprisoned or exiled, God has stationed us where we are for His good and His glory. Jesus himself told us we would have trouble in this world in John 16:33. No where are we ever told that life, and certainly not ministry, will be easy. But it is worth it.

The last part of John 16:33 is Jesus telling us not to worry about the trouble in this life, because he has overcome this world. As we faithfully serve, work with excellence, and hold tightly to the promises of victory that Christ has for us, we will see God bring joy through pain and peace through adversity.

Just because you *feel* like you are imprisoned is no reason to give up. Push ahead. Work diligently. Do everything with excellence. And then you will see God move in ways you would never have expected.

Hold Fast

What promises are there in Psalm 146:7?

Stay True

What are the issues that re causing you to feel like you are in prison?

Is it an issue with senior leadership?

Are you feeling overlooked and underappreciated?

Thought: Be honest about where the emotions are coming from. It is impossible to deal with these issues without being brutally honest.

How is your circumstance impacting your performance in your ministry?

Are you still doing your work with excellence?

Are you simply trying to get through the day?

How is it impacting your family life?

Who can you discuss these issues with in. a safe environment?

Is there someone outside your ministry context you can share honestly with?

 Is there a danger to your job if you have honest discussions about these issues with our supervisors?

Chapter 8 - Promotion

"If God qualifies you, nothing else can disqualify you." Matshona Dhliwayo

Joseph was brought from the prison to the palace to interpret Pharaoh's dream. As we discussed in the previous chapter, Joseph takes no credit or glory for himself but instead gives God all the glory for his gift. How often do we, not pridefully or with intent, steal glory from God? It happens in many unconscious ways.

When an event goes well, how often do we take credit for our awesome planning, attention to detail, and creative mindset? Or when we knock it out of the park speaking, when someone says, Great job," do we respond with, "thank you." It may seem innocent, but there is an aspect where we steal God's glory when we don't specifically put him at the center.

I have a friend who is an amazing communicator. He has given some of the best, most creative talks I have ever heard. He is a guy who, in my opinion, is going to become a nationally known commodity very soon. I often text him after I have heard him speak and tell him what a great job he did. His reply is ALWAYS, "Praise God."

It may seem like no big deal, but I think one of the reasons for Joseph's success in the eyes of his captors was that he gave the glory to God. In Genesis 41:16, as we looked at before, when Joseph is told by Pharaoh that he has heard he can interpret dreams, Joseph responds with,

> *"It is beyond my power to do, but God can tell you what it means and set your mind at ease."*

Sometimes we must recognize what is beyond ourselves and what we must rely on God's power to accomplish. Yes, our gifts, our faithfulness, and our excellence in our work will gain human attention. But at the end of the day, everything we could possibly bring to the table is a direct result of God's blessing on our lives.

Let's put ourselves in Joseph's shoes for a moment. At 17 he is sold into slavery. He ends up at Potiphar's house and serves for over a decade, where he is given charge of the entire house. Then, he goes to prison for at least two years. Again, he is put in charge of the entire prison. This kind of turns the adage the "prisoners running the asylum," on its ear! Then, at 30 years old, he is brought before the absolute ruler of Egypt to interpret his dreams. Can you see how this might throw off our equilibrium a touch?

Think back on your life and ministry. Are you where you thought you would be at this point? For many of us, we could not have imagined we would end up here.

If you are in a good, healthy, supportive ministry, you probably did not expect things to turn out as well as they have. If you find yourself in a place of exile, or even a prison, you probably never thought it could get this bad.

Years ago, I was feeling worn out in ministry. I had been through an incredibly difficult season in the church I was leading. As I mentioned before, my best friend had committed adultery, and we had to practice church discipline. This was while we were in the middle of our building project, which he was overseeing. Another leader in the church picked up that project, and two months later, he and his wife met me for lunch and told me they were leaving the church. When the building was finally complete, I was wiped out.

No one offered a sabbatical or an extended break. I simply knew that I needed to get out of my routine and let my brain and heart heal. I also knew that sitting on a beach or just hanging out somewhere was not the answer. So, I heard about it and registered for a trip all in one day. It was not for a cruise or an all-inclusive getaway, but it was literally to go and dig dirt for ten days in Haiti.

I had never been to Haiti before and honestly had no desire to go. But when I found this trip, it struck a chord. I was going to an area I knew nothing about, with people I knew nothing about, to do mindless digging. When I told my wife what I was doing when I got home, her response was a shocked, "You're doing what?"

I couldn't even answer her basic questions with anything that would make her feel at ease. "Who are you going with?" "Some people I heard about online." "Do you know any of the people going?" "No." "Why do you want to go do this?" "I don't know."

I went on the trip, and it was awesome. I didn't know anyone and knew nothing about any details of the trip. No one asked me any logistical questions the entire time I was there. Every day, our group would head to a hill in another village from where the mission was, and we would dig for hours at a time. In the evening, we would visit with one another and the mission staff. I began to develop a connection with the Director of the mission, and we became good friends. He began to tell me some of the history of the place and the people. It was fascinating. And about three years later, I would find myself leaving the church I was pastoring to work for the mission I had visited simply to get away from the stress of my life for a week.

I never thought my life would be dedicated to ministry. I never thought we would leave our church in California for Florida. I never thought I would go from student ministry to a senior pastor role. I never thought I would have to deal with my best friend's sin. I never thought I would leave a local church to work in the mission field. And I never thought I would go back into student ministry and feel so satisfied in my life.

But I firmly believe that God had me on this path, just as he had Joseph on his path. If I had never worked in the church in California, I would never have fallen in love with working with students. If I had stayed in the church in California, I don't think they would have ever seen me as the senior pastor, but as the 21-year-old youth guy. If I had not gone through the challenges in leadership I experienced in my first church in Florida, I would not have had the understanding to lead a staff at a church when I became the lead pastor. And if I had not served in Haiti, my heart and compassion for others would not be as tender as it is.

I heard a message the other day on the life of Joseph. While I am in the midst of writing this book, my home church is doing a series on Joseph. One of the speakers a few weeks ago made a statement that caught my attention. She said, "Joseph did not see himself stranded in slavery or in prison. Instead, he saw himself as stationed there." In other words, Joseph saw that God had placed him in all of these places for a purpose. Wherever he was, Joseph put his head down, did his work with excellence, and God blessed him. Because of Joseph's perspective, God was able to promote him.

After he interprets Pharaoh's dream, Joseph is literally put in charge of the nation of Egypt. From slave to ruler in a little over a decade. Did Joseph know he was headed in that direction? Of course not! Joseph probably felt like he could never catch a break. And when he did catch a break, he always ended up in a worse situation.

Think about it this way: Joseph is a favored son and is given a beautiful coat by his father to show his love for Joseph. This does not sit well with his brothers, who want to kill him but instead decide to sell him off as a slave. He ends up in Egypt at Potiphar's house and rises to being the manager of the house of the man in charge of the Egyptian military. He is falsely accused and sent to prison. He ends up running the entire prison. While in prison, he helps another prisoner who gets restored to his job. He thinks that he will be remembered and that he will be freed from prison. Only to spend another year in prison. Then he is brought before Pharaoh.

Joseph had no idea that Pharaoh would put him in charge of Egypt. After he interprets the dream and lays out a plan to save Egypt, he finds himself, once again, in a place he never expected. I picture Joseph going to bed that first night out of prison and thinking, "When is the other shoe going to fall?"

But in this moment, Joseph has not only been promoted by Pharaoh, but he has been promoted by God. While he doesn't know exactly what will occur, at least we are never told he knows; he must sense that God is doing something he could not imagine.

During this period in his life, Joseph marries for the first time and has two sons. In Genesis 41:50-52, we read,

> *"During this time, before the first of the famine years, two sons were born to Joseph and his wife, Asenath, the daughter of Potiphera, the priest of On.* [51] *Joseph named his older son Manasseh, for he said, "God has made me forget all my troubles and everyone in my father's family."* [52] *Joseph named his second son Ephraim, for he said, "God has made me fruitful in this land of my grief."*

Did you catch the meaning of Joseph's sons' names? Manasseh means "God has made me forget my troubles and everyone in my father's family." Every day, for 13 years, Joseph has been reminded of the troubles his family caused. I can imagine that not a day went by that he did not look at his circumstance and think, "What if?"

His second son, Ephraim, means, "God has made me fruitful in the land of my grief." This tells us that Joseph did not have a happy life in Egypt. It is sometimes easy to think that the people mentioned in scripture went through their trials and their circumstances with ease. But what we see here is that Joseph walked through Egypt in grief. It was only when he was promoted and placed in his position by Potiphar that we are told the grief begins to lift.

While we may think Joseph has arrived and everything is rosy and wonderful, remember the nation of Egypt, and in fact, we are told the entire world (Genesis 41:57) is going through seven years of famine. Joseph had prepped the nation for this catastrophe, but it is still not a pleasant or easy situation.

When the people cry out to Pharaoh for food, he sends them to Joseph. The crowds all come to him to provide for their needs. Have you ever been around hungry teenagers? They are like velociraptors about to take your head off for a snack. Now, picture the entire nation, and people from surrounding nations who are literally starving to death.

In ministry, we always assume that once we are in the position, we have arrived. I am the head of a large student ministry; I have made it! I am the director of this mission or that non-profit; I have arrived. I am now the senior pastor; I am King!! Okay, that may be a little exaggerated. The point is, promotion does not mean ease.

When I have trained leaders in ministry, one of the things I try to instill in them is that ministry leadership comes with only one right. It's not the right to a bigger office. It's not the right to your own parking place (don't get me started), and it is not the right to ease up on your work. The only right the ministry gives you is the right to be inconvenienced.

Whatever your role or status in ministry, your rights are not the central factor or focus. I have heard repeatedly about my right to do this or my right to say that. When we become followers of Jesus, we must kill the idea of our rights to certain liberties for the right to serve the King of the Universe. That doesn't mean we become doormats and allow people to walk all over us. But it means that at the end of the day, we are in the role of a servant more than we are the role of being served.

One of my treasured mementos in my office is a small white golf towel that was given to me when I graduated from International School of Theology (ISOT). ISOT was founded by Bill Bright as an education arm for Campus Crusade for Christ. It was designed originally to train Campus Crusade staff biblically. Over time it became an accredited seminary and opened to the public.

Upon graduation, each of us were given a towel with the ISOT crest embroidered on it. During our commencement ceremony, Dr. Bright reminded us that ministry was about a towel, no matter the position we held. He referenced Jesus washing the disciples' feet and the call for us to do the same. Whenever I see that towel, I am reminded of the fact that Jesus washed feet on the night before he died for my sins. What could possibly be more important for me than to serve those for whom Jesus died?

Joseph's promotion in Egypt was not all about him. Instead, he understood that through him, God was going to save millions of people. His promotion was not about his comfort, but his service. Yes, he had perks. He had servants, he lived in a palace, and he directed the affairs of the nation. But at the end of the day, he was still a foreigner in a foreign land who had risen from slavery to the palace for a purpose bigger than himself.

Hold Fast

Read 1 Samuel 24.

What lessons do you see about power from title, and power from authority?

Stay True

Where are the "never imagined" places in your life?

How did you end up there?

Were there lessons that you learned along the way?

Thought: God works in our "never imagined" spaces. Don't miss the lessons along the way.

What "promotion" are you hoping to receive?

What will it take to get there?

Chapter 8 - Promotion

What steps are you taking to make it happen?

Thought: It's good and healthy for us to have goals and dreams. Make sure your goals and dreams line up with the heart of God for your life.

Chapter 9- Forgiveness

"To forgive is to set a prisoner free, and to realize the prisoner is you."

Lewis Smedes

Have you ever been wronged? I don't mean someone-cut-you-off-in-traffic-wronged, I mean someone close to you deeply hurt you and scarred your life forever. We have a foolish thought in our culture that it is somehow possible to "forgive and forget" when people hurt us. We can forgive, in fact, it is required, but it is almost impossible for us to forget.

Scars are a reminder of pain. Last year, I had a pain in my elbow that I couldn't explain. It started as just an ache, and then it began to swell. When I finally went to the doctor, X-rays showed that I had a broken bone in my elbow. I had no idea how I had done that. There was a piece of bone floating in my elbow that was causing pain and swelling. I had to have surgery on my elbow, and I have a scar to prove it.

As I think about that experience, I see how my elbow injury and pain reflect the pain of unforgiveness. We know something is wrong. We know there is an issue, but we don't know how or why it is impacting our lives. Like an unseen broken bone, unforgiveness irritates us at the deepest level until it is fully removed.

The emotional scars on our hearts often reflect a far greater pain than the physical scars. When we have scars on the inside of our lives, they have been placed there by others whom we believed we could trust. They come from the people we loved the most and who we believed loved us.

Almost twenty years have passed since Joseph was betrayed and sold into slavery by his brothers. You know the story. A famine sweeps through the entire region, and Jacob sends his sons to Egypt to find food to save the family. When Joseph first encounters his brothers, we are told,

> *"Although Joseph recognized his brothers, they didn't recognize him. 9 And he remembered the dreams he'd had about them many years before...."*
>
> *Genesis 42:8-9*

Imagine all the thoughts going through Joseph's mind. The times around a fire where the family told stories of God's faithfulness. Times when he and Benjamin, being the youngest children, laughed and enjoyed the innocence of childhood. The pain of his brothers grabbing him. The injuries from the pit. The look on their faces as the traders took him away to a foreign land. Joy, excitement, betrayal, pain all in one instance. Scars.

What do we do when we are confronted with the person who caused pain and harm in our life? What is the proper response? Not the Sunday School answer of, "we forgive," but the real, honest, unfiltered emotions and words that flow when we have been wronged. We have options.

Corrie Ten Boom was a Dutch young lady caught during World War II. She and her family had helped to hide Jews from the Nazi's and were caught and sent to concentration camps. Corrie and her sister, Betsie, were sent to Ravensbrück, a harsh place where thousands and thousands of Jews lost their lives. The guards were cruel, and the conditions were filthy. Corrie survived the war, but Betsie did not.

After the war, Corrie began to speak and teach throughout Europe of God's love. On one occasion, and man stayed behind to meet her. This is her account of that night:

It was in a church in Munich that I saw him, a balding, heavyset man in a gray overcoat, a brown felt hat clutched between his hands. People were filing out of the basement room where I had just spoken, moving along the rows of wooden chairs to the door at the rear. It was 1947, and I had come from Holland to defeated Germany with the message that God forgives. It was the truth they needed most to hear in that bitter, bombed-out land, and I gave them my favorite mental picture. Maybe because the sea is never far from a Hollander's mind, I liked to think that that's where forgiven sins were thrown. "When we confess our sins," I said, "God casts them into the deepest ocean, gone forever."

The solemn faces stared back at me, not quite daring to believe. There were no questions after a talk in Germany in 1947. People stood up in silence, collected their wraps in silence, and left the room.

And that's when I saw him, working his way forward against the others. One moment, I saw the overcoat and the brown hat: the next, a blue uniform and a visored cap with its skull and crossbones.

It came back with a rush: the huge room with its harsh overhead lights, the pathetic pile of dresses and shoes in the center of the floor, the shame of walking naked past this man. I could see my sister's frail form ahead of me, ribs sharp beneath the parchment skin. Betsie, how thin you were!

Betsie and I had been arrested for concealing Jews in our home during the Nazi occupation of Holland; this man had been a guard at Ravensbrück concentration camp, where we were sent.

Now he was in front of me, hand thrust out: "A fine message, *fräulein*! How good it is to know that, as you say, all our sins are at the bottom of the sea!" And I, who had spoken so glibly of forgiveness, fumbled in my pocketbook rather than take that hand. He would not remember me, of course–how could he remember one prisoner among those thousands of women?

But I remembered him and the leather crop swinging from his belt. It was the first time since my release that I had been face-to-face with one of my captors, and my blood seemed to freeze. "You mentioned Ravensbrück in your talk," he was saying. "I was a guard in there." No, he did not remember me. "But since that time," he went on, "I have become a Christian. I know that God has forgiven me for the cruel things I did there, but I would like to hear it from your lips as well. *Fräulein*"–again the hand came out– "will you forgive me?"

And I stood there–I whose sins had every day to be forgiven–and could not. Betsie had died in that place– could he erase her slow, terrible death simply for the asking?

It could not have been many seconds that he stood there, hand held out, but to me it seemed hours as I wrestled with the most difficult thing I had ever had to do.

For I had to do it–I knew that. The message that God forgives has a prior condition: that we forgive those who have injured us. "If you do not forgive men their trespasses," Jesus says, "neither will your Father in heaven forgive your trespasses."

I knew it not only as a commandment of God, but as a daily experience. Since the end of the war, I had had a home in Holland for victims of Nazi brutality.

Those who were able to forgive their former enemies were able also to return to the outside world and rebuild their lives, no matter what the physical scars. Those who nursed their bitterness remained invalids. It was as simple and as horrible as that.

And still I stood there with the coldness clutching my heart. But forgiveness is not an emotion–I knew that too. Forgiveness is an act of the will, and the will can function regardless of the temperature of the heart.

"Jesus, help me!" I prayed silently. "I can lift my hand. I can do that much. You supply the feeling."

And so woodenly, mechanically, I thrust my hand into the one stretched out to me. And as I did, an incredible thing took place. The current started in my shoulder, raced down my arm, sprang into our joined hands. And then this healing warmth seemed to flood my whole being, bringing tears to my eyes.

> *"I forgive you, brother!" I cried. "With all my heart!" (Guideposts, November 1972)*

I cannot imagine what I would have done in that situation. Would I have been willing to seek the Lord's help to forgive? I would hope so, but honestly, I do not know. There is a powerful truth within this small story that I don't want us to miss.

Corrie said that since the war she had run a house in Holland for survivors of the Holocaust. She noticed a remarkable difference in those who were able to forgive their captors and those who could not. Those who were able to forgive went on to "normal" lives. They held jobs, had families, and contributed to society. Those who held onto bitterness and rage, remained, in her words, invalids.

Over the next few chapters, we see Joseph playing a game of espionage with his brothers. He calls them spies and throws them into prison. He releases them, keeping one in prison until they return with their little brother. Then they say the thing that it seems no one has dared utter for twenty years.

> *"Speaking among themselves, they said, "Clearly, we are being punished because of what we did to Joseph long ago. We saw his anguish when he pleaded for his life, but we wouldn't listen. That's why we're in this trouble."* **22** *"Didn't I tell you not to sin against the boy?" Reuben asked. "But you wouldn't listen. And now we have to answer for his blood!" Genesis 42:21-22*

Joseph has been listening to them speak, although they did not know he could understand them. He had a translator to continue the act. But when they attribute their present condition to how they treated him, he is overwhelmed with emotion.

You have endured the life of betrayal, exile, enslavement, prison, and have risen to power, and now the people who put in motion your entire existence realize they treated you wrongly and believe they are being judged by God. It would be the natural human emotion to lash out. No one would blame Joseph if he stood and shouted, "Don't you know who I am!! You ruined my entire life!!" And because of his rank and position, we would expect him to get revenge.

But Joseph has another narrative in mind. In fact, his plans and his actions are the first recorded instances of forgiveness in scripture. God alludes to forgiveness in Genesis 3, but that is a distant promise of a coming Messiah. Until Joseph, scripture is filled with getting even, getting back, punishment, and reward. Nowhere is forgiveness expressed in human form until Joseph interacts with his brothers.

Haven't we all thought about how to get back at those who hurt us? I have pictured in my mind what I would like to say, or more precisely shout, at those who hurt me. I have imagined the feeling of hearing them say, you were right. I have pictured the feeling of triumph to having the wrongs righted.

But just as Corrie Ten Boom had to recognize that she must be forgiven daily, I have had to recognize that unforgiveness on my part is not a Christlike virtue. In honesty, I have allowed unforgiveness to live in my heart for far too long in many instances. And it has its consequences.

Unforgiveness has a crippling effect on our lives. It not only impacts our soul and our mind, but it can also cause physical trauma as well. According to a Johns Hopkins study, unforgiveness causes anxiety, stress, high blood pressure, and severe depression. Forgiveness, on the other hand, lowers blood pressure, lessens anxiety, and reduces stress.

Forgiveness also has a spiritual healing that it brings to the table. When we forgive, we are never more like our Heavenly Father. God had no need to forgive us. It is not as if he was unable to move on or couldn't carry out his job because we had turned our backs on him. However, he chose to forgive purely out of his own love.

When we forgive, we are acting within a system that God created and perfected. Forgiveness is not a human idea or mandate. We humans are far more apt to seek revenge and evenness than we are forgiving. But there is another way that we are shown in scripture.

> *"Make allowance for each other's faults and forgive anyone who offends you. Remember, the Lord forgave you, so you must forgive others." Colossians 3:15*

Because we have been forgiven, we are required to forgive others. It is not a suggestion or a hint, but a command. That causes a deep hesitation to think about the implications of unforgiveness.

My sins, placed and paid for at the cross of Jesus, and yet an unkind word, an unprovoked attack, or a casual slight cause us to hold onto bitterness and contempt for others who have been forgiven by Christ.

When Christ forgives, it is complete, and it is lasting. It is not something that is rehashed repeatedly with friends. It is not something that God brings up to hold against us. God's forgiveness is as if he has forgotten it completely, although. We know God does not forget.

> *"And I will forgive their wickedness, and I will never again remember their sins."*
>
> *Jeremiah 31:34*

We know that God is omniscient. That means He always knows everything. So how in the world could a God who knows all things always forget our sins? The passage doesn't say he forgets our sins. It says he chooses to remember them no more. God willingly puts our sins away and never puts them in front of us for our shame.

Alana and I have been married 35 years. In those 35 years, I can't imagine how many times I have been unkind, short-tempered, frustrated, and simply downright rude. But there has never been one time that Alana has been angry with me and said, "Do you remember when you did ....." That is the image of how God forgives us. I am sure Alana remembers times when I sinned against her. But she chooses to never use it against me.

When Joseph encounters his brothers, he is moved to tears. In Genesis 45, Joseph finally reveals who his to his brothers. As he does, they are left speechless. But Joseph makes a statement that is, in my opinion, one of the most biblical, theologically sound arguments. He says...

> *"But don't be upset, and don't be angry with yourselves for selling me to this place. It was God who sent me here ahead of you to preserve your lives."*
>
> *Genesis 45:5*

Joseph, through all the pain, all the scars, and all the memories of betrayal recognizes the sovereignty of God and releases his brothers from the burden of their sin. When we see the circumstances of our lives as divinely appointed, we are able to move past the human element and into the forgiving nature of God.

I look at my life and can see times where I have been hurt, wronged, and even betrayed. In those moments, those experiences were painful and caused me to have more questions than answers. But in hindsight, those moments were God-ordained circumstances that caused me to grow physically, spiritually, mentally, and emotionally.

> *Dear brothers and sisters, when troubles of any kind come your way, consider it an opportunity for great joy. 3 For you know that when your faith is tested, your*

endurance has a chance to grow. 4 So let it grow, for when your endurance is fully developed, you will be perfect and complete, needing nothing."

James 1:2-4

While we go through the "troubles of any kind," we see the ugliness of a fallen world. We experience life as it was never intended because humanity is sinful from birth. On the opposite side of our hurt, are seasons of forgiveness, endurance, and growth. We would not know the blessing of the growth and maturity it we did not first walk through the pain.

In dealing with the issues I experienced with my mom, I was able to make choices in how I parented my children. I was able to be more present, more open, and more honest. In dealing with leaders who have hurt me in church life, I have learned to be a better leader and pastor. When I have felt betrayed, I have learned to be more understanding of the brokenness inside those who caused the pain.

I have always found the end of Joseph's story with his brothers to be fascinating. After all the time, all the conversations, all the help Joseph gave to save his family, they still did not fully believe him. After Jacob dies, his brothers believe that Joseph will kill them and finally get his revenge. They don't trust that Joseph can truly forgive.

One reason Joseph's brothers could not believe Joseph could forgive them is, in my opinion, that they could not forgive themselves. The person we find it hardest to forgive is ourselves. We harbor all of the pain we caused, we remember every sinful detail, and we replay every experience repeatedly. Literally, just this morning, I woke up thinking of how I hurt someone over 35 years go. I remembered the shame of my sin and was almost brought to tears.

Forgiving ourselves is not letting ourselves off the hook. Instead, it is placing ourselves under the blood of Jesus and "remembering no more." Those thoughts may creep into our mind, but we must not let them take up residence. We must remind ourselves that our sin, just like everyone who has come to faith is Christ, was paid for at the cross.

The other reason I believe they had a hard time believing Joseph, was that forgiveness was not a quality to be admired in the ancient world. Remember, this is pre-law, pre-scripture, and pre-grace. This was an eye-for-an-eye world. But Joseph, because of his deep faith and trust in God, credits God for these events. Therefore, he frees his brothers from the human punishment of their sin.

> "But Joseph replied, "Don't be afraid of me. Am I God, that I can punish you? [20] You intended to harm me, but God intended it all for good. He brought me to this position so I could save the lives of many

people. 21 No, don't be afraid. I will continue to take care of you and your children." So he reassured them by speaking kindly to them."

Genesis 50:19-21

If his brothers were to be punished, Joseph knew it was best to let God do the punishing. Joseph, despite all the wrongs done to him, chooses God's sovereign plan over his own human vengeance.

How often are we guilty of wanting revenge? How often are we afraid that those who hurt us will go unpunished? Honestly, how often are we afraid that God will extend grace to those who sinned against us?

Whatever we have gone through, God has seen it, been present with us in it, and gives us the power to overcome it. But we must first believe that what man "intended to harm" God intended for good.

When we fully understand the grace and goodness of God, despite our circumstances, we can begin to stay true to the call of God in our lives. If we don't get forgiveness correct, we will live in the murky waters of bitterness. We will minister and serve out of cracked vessels, instead of jars of clay that have been strengthened by our Heavenly Father.

This last section of the story of Joseph may be the most challenging to live out. It may be where we need to stay and meditate for a long period of time. Forgiveness is not easy, and it is never cheap. Remember, our forgiveness required the death of the only perfect person to ever live. It required a loving Father to give his only son, in order that we may have eternal life. Forgiveness is not easy, but it is worth it.

Hold Fast

What do you learn about forgiveness from Colossians 3:13

Stay True

Who do you need to forgive? Why do you need to forgive this person?

Who do you need to ask forgiveness from? Why do you need to be forgiven?

What is holding you back from extending forgiveness?

Chapter 10- Now What?

"People have the unique ability to hear one story and understand another."

Pandora Poikilos

We began at the end of Joseph's story, and here we are placing understanding into our own story. Lessons learned from others can be motivating, heart-warming, cautionary, or educational. My prayer is that as you have journeyed with me through the story of Joseph, myself, and others, you have found all of the above. I pray you are motivated to not give up in your walk with God or your calling from God. I pray you have been encouraged by some of the stories of God's faithfulness through pain. I pray that you have learned that there are areas in our lives where we need to practice caution to be successful. And I pray you have learned some new strategies and insights along the way.

This work was born of pain. I have shared my own pain and the pain of others. I desire that the pain you have experienced in the past, that you are walking through now, or that you will face in the future, will have a growing and maturing impact on your life. DON'T WASTE YOUR PAIN.

I have two sections to share to finish out this work. One is filled with insight and wisdom from some of my best friends in ministry. Some have been friends for decades, and some have been friends for a couple of years. But each one is a faithful minister of Christ who has served at least fifteen years in ministry.

Wisdom From the Field

> *"Your first calling is to Christ, not to ministry."*-

Jonathan Samuels

Above your ministry, your title, or your position, your first call is as a Child of God. We must always remember that to be a good leader, you must first be a faithful follower of Christ. Our anchor in our ministry is our relationship with Christ, not a title or role.

> *"You must have a confirmation of your calling in ministry."*

Jonathan Samuels

Ministry should not be a job or profession. Ministry is a result of a call of God on your life. All Christians are called to minister, but not all are called to vocational ministry. If you do not have confirmation of your calling from God, from your ministry leaders, and from those whom you are leading, you will not last long in vocational ministry. When you are confident in your call, you can persevere through the hard times.

"Instead of striving for balance, fight for health."

Jody Livingston

Balance is a myth in our culture. There are only so many hours in a day, and there are endless ways we can spend those hours. To keep from burning out, find a healthy rhythm for your life. Find healthy rhythms for your family, your rest, and your health. This will look different for everyone, and it will change as the seasons of your life change, but you must be the one who fights for your health.

"You are replaceable at work; you are not replaceable at home."

Jay Holland

Whether you burn out, flame out, or check out in ministry, your church will find another person to fill your role. But your family cannot find another you. God gave you a spouse and children that you are responsible for above everything else. That doesn't mean we never work hard or have long hours, but it means we don't align the church as the first importance in our lives.

"Approach ministry as if you are going to be there 10-15 years."

Jay Holland

Have a plan of ministry and grow the people you are leading with a long-term view in mind. You need a strategy of ministry and a routine of life that allows you to invest in others. If God calls you to move or step out of an area, you will have invested strategically and purposefully into others.

> *"Use the lessons God has taught you to pour into others."*

Todd Pearage

God shows each of us different lessons throughout our lives that we need, but that are also needed by others. No matter your age or experience, you can pour into someone who is coming behind you. Don't keep the lessons to yourself but invest them in others.

> *"Above all else, spend time with Jesus."*

Mike Skillman

We minister and serve out of the overflow of our own hearts and souls. If we are only in the Word to prepare, we will find our own hearts empty. We must spend time with Jesus in our own lives for our own growth.

Thoughts for the Church Leaders

I want to close with some thoughts for leaders in high-level capacities at their ministries. You have been entrusted with great responsibility from God. You are in a role of not only leading the ministry God has called you to lead, but also to shepherd those who God has placed in your organization. How you do this reflects your heart and your soul. Here are some thoughts on how you can help those in your organization last for the long haul.

Confirm the Call

For people to last in ministry, those who oversee them in ministry need to help them discern and confirm the call of God on their lives. If they are seeking a paycheck and a job, they will struggle with the spiritual challenges that come with ministry.

If churches can help younger pastors and leaders discern the clarity of call on their lives, they can help them see a longer vision of growth and ministry. Unfortunately, churches are often focused on results and leadership instead of clarity and calling.

Prepare Them for Challenges

Spiritual battles and challenges are part of every Christian's life, but it is exponentially intensified for those in ministry. People need to understand that struggles are part of ministry life. If we allow discouragement to become the norm, we will see people lose vision, passion, and joy in ministry.

Lead Through Failures

People fail. It is true of everyone, in every job, and every walk of life. Often, churches see failure as a lack of maturity and growth. We actually learn more from failure than we do from success. When we fail, we look deeper at the issues, we strive to learn, and we seek input from those with experience.

I have often seen churches use failure as a weapon instead of an opportunity. You did not reach your level of leadership without some failures. Remember what it was like to fail and help people fail forward. Failure is not final, and it is seldom fatal.

Shepherd Rather Than Supervise

When churches hire people, they often view them as someone to supervise. What we need to remember is that churches need to shepherd their own staff. They are going to have struggles. Every temptation that every person in your church faces, your staff will face, sometimes at greater levels. That doesn't excuse sin, but it should help us to see the spiritual condition over the work condition.

Pastors are people. Failure in areas is going to happen. If possible, when there is repentance, see restoration. Maybe they need to be sent to some intense counseling. Maybe they need to go to a retreat with their spouse. Maybe they need to be given some time to step back in ministry and work on their own souls. Whatever the church can do, we should seek to bring health and restoration to those who serve.

Seek Health

Far too often, churches see capable, willing, and valuable people, and we hand off more and more responsibilities to those same people. When we continue to give responsibilities, we dilute effectiveness in areas of expertise. The people who are excellent up front may not have great administrative skills. People who are detail-oriented and task-oriented may not lead teams well. We need to look at how we can come alongside them and help them use their gifts and talents in the most effective ways possible.

We also need to understand the rhythms of life. When we ask people to give up time over and over again, we are asking them to work in unhealthy rhythms. That is sustainable for a short time, but in the long run, we are telling them we are more concerned with our programs than our people. Don't let programs destroy your people.

I want to remind you, once again, as we close, that the purpose of this book is to help you last for the long haul. The message of Joseph may resonate with you. The personal stories shared may strike a chord in your heart. Whatever it is, I encourage you to trust God to bring to light what is hidden and bring healing to what is broken.

I want to remind you of what was said in the beginning.....

Jesus died for the church, so you don't have to.

Our call is to faithfully follow Jesus, minister first to our family and second to those God has entrusted to our care, and third to finish well. Don't give up. The journey is long and at times incredibly difficult, but there is no higher calling than serving the King of the Universe faithfully.

Hold Fast! Stay True! God is still on the throne, and He is not finished with you yet!

If you find yourself in deep hurt and don't know where to go, here are a few resources to guide you:

Standing Stone Ministry is a ministry designed to guide ministry leaders into healthy ministry. Free counseling resources for ministry leaders and their families.

www.standingstoneminsitry.org

Care For Pastors is a safe place for pastors, their spouses, and their kids. This ministry, located in Leesburg, Florida, has options for help over web-based meetings or in person. www.careforpastors.org

And if you just need a listening ear and a prayer partner, you can reach me at John@johnharveyofficial.com.

Sources

Chapter 1

When Harry Met Sally, directed by Rob Reiner (1989, United States, Castle Rock Productions)

Chapter 2

Lilo and Stitch, directed by Dean DeBlois and Chris Sanders (2002, United States and Japan, Walt Disney Productions)

Andy Stanley, *Choosing to Cheat* (Nashville: Thomas Nelson, 2002), 21

Marilee Pierce Dunker, *Man of Vision*, (California: Marliee Pierce Dunker, 2010)

Chapter 3

Thomas Merton, *No Man is An Island* (Boston: Mariner Books, 2002), 106ff

Chapter 4

Emily Van Gordon

Shinobu Kitayama and Jiyoung Park, *Science Direct, Emotion and biological health: the socio-cultural moderation*

Chapter 5

Marco Rubio, USA Today, 2012

Chapter 6

Oscar Wilde, *Lady Windermere's Fan,* (London, 1893)

C.S. Lewis, *The Lion, The Witch, and The Wardrobe* (London: Geoffry Bes, 1950), 34-37

Ibid, 181-182

Chapter 7

The Count of Monte Cristo, directed by Kevin Reynolds (2002; United States: Touchstone Pictures)

Chapter 8

Matshona Dhliwayo, African Leadership Magazine

Chapter 9

Sources

Lewis Smedes, Forgive and Forget: Healing the Hurts we Don't Deserve (New York: Harper Collins, 2007)

Corrie Ten Boom, Guideposts, 1972

Chapter 10

Pandora Paikilos, Excuse Me, My Brains Have Stepped Out (CreateSpace, Independent Publishing Platform, 2012)

About the Author

John Harvey has been in full-time ministry for the past 36 years. He has served the local church as a student pastor, associate pastor, lead pastor, and missionary.

John is currently a Regional Director for First Priority of South Florida, taking the gospel of Christ to students on public school campuses.

He and his wife, Alana, have three adult biological children, Emily, Zach, and Kimberly, and one bonus blessing daughter, Dani. They live with their dog, Dixie, in Port St. Lucie, FL.